T0252901

Macintosh Terminal
Pocket Guide

Daniel J. Barrett

Beijing · Cambridge · Farnham · Köln · Sebastopol · Tokyo

Macintosh Terminal Pocket Guide
by Daniel J. Barrett

Copyright © 2012 Daniel Barrett. All rights reserved.
Printed in the United States of America.

Published by O'Reilly Media, Inc., 1005 Gravenstein Highway North, Sebastopol, CA 95472.

O'Reilly books may be purchased for educational, business, or sales promotional use. Online editions are also available for most titles (*http://my.safari booksonline.com*). For more information, contact our corporate/institutional sales department: 800-998-9938 or *corporate@oreilly.com*.

Editors: Mike Loukides and Andy Oram
Production Editor: Iris Febres
Proofreader: Kiel Van Horn
Indexer: Daniel Barrett
Cover Designer: Karen Montgomery
Interior Designer: David Futato
Illustrators: Robert Romano and Rebecca Demarest

June 2012:   First Edition.

Revision History for the First Edition:
2012-06-11	First release
2012-07-13	Second release
2012-12-14	Third release

See *http://oreilly.com/catalog/errata.csp?isbn=9781449328344* for release details.

ISBN: 978-1-449-32834-4

[LSI]

1355165754

Contents

CHAPTER 1

The Macintosh Terminal

Welcome to the Macintosh's best-kept secret: the Terminal! If you've ever browsed the *Utilities* folder, you've probably seen this icon:

Terminal

Maybe you've even launched the Terminal and seen a plain, dull-looking window appear, displaying mysterious words:

But if you're like most users, this is probably as far as you've explored. And that is a shame, because the Terminal is one of the most powerful programs for controlling your Mac.

What is the Terminal? What does it do? And why should you care? Let's answer the last question by telling a few stories:

- You're running Microsoft Word for the Mac when its window suddenly freezes. You type, but nothing happens. You try to quit Word, but it doesn't respond. In desperation, you go to the application dock, select the Word icon, and choose "Force Quit." Even this has no effect! You are stuck and have no choice but to reboot your Mac.

- You have a folder of 1,000 PDF files named *file1*, *file2*, *file3*, and so on. For compatibility with a coworker's computer, you need to rename these files to have *.pdf* extensions. The Finder doesn't seem to have any way to perform these renames in bulk, so you do them one file at a time (click, click, click) until your hands cramp.

- Last week, you copied a *huge* folder of files (and all its subfolders, 10 levels deep) from your Mac to a server on your network. The transfer took over an hour. During the next few days, you modified a few dozen of the original files, and now you want to copy the changed files to the remote server. Of course, you don't want to copy the entire folder again and wait a whole hour! You want to copy just the files that have changed. Unfortunately, you didn't keep track of which ones you modified, so you hunt them down and copy them one by one...which ends up taking even longer than an hour.

Do these stories sound familiar? In each case, there seems to be no simple solution using the Mac Finder, and you wind up wasting time: rebooting, clicking icons one by one, or hunting through large folders by hand. Well, we have good news. These problems are all *easily solved* by typing and running commands in the Terminal. In fact, here are the commands that solve our three problems:

```
killall -KILL 'Microsoft Word'        Terminate Word

for i in file*; do mv $i $i.pdf; done  Rename your PDFs

rsync -aE myfolder server:             Copy changed files
```

These short, somewhat cryptic commands get the job done quickly. The Terminal can save you minutes, hours, or even days of work if you learn the right commands. That's what this book is all about.

By the way, if you're a system administrator of multiple OS X computers, you're going to love the Terminal. Its command line is outstanding for automating system tasks.

What's in This Book?

This book is a short guide to the Terminal, *not a comprehensive reference*. We cover important, useful aspects of the Terminal (and its partner, the "shell") so you can work productively. We do not, however, present every single command and every last option (our apologies if your favorite was omitted), nor delve into detail about OS X internals. Short, sweet, and essential, that's our motto.

We focus on *commands*, the words typed on a command line to tell your Macintosh what to do. Here's an example command that counts lines of text in a file, *myfile*:

```
wc -l myfile
```

We'll cover the most important commands for the average user, such as `ls` (list files), `grep` (search for text in a file), `kill` (terminate programs), and `df` (measure free disk space), plus some advanced commands like `dscl` (manage users and groups) and `launchctl` (run services and scheduled jobs). We assume you are already familiar with the Mac desktop and the Finder.

We've organized the material by function to provide a concise learning path. For example, to help you view the contents of a file, we introduce all file-viewing commands together: `cat` for short text files, `less` for longer ones, `od` for binary files, and so on. Then we explain each command in turn, briefly presenting its common uses and options.

At press time, the current version of OS X is Lion (10.7).

What's the Terminal?

The Terminal is an application that runs commands. If you're familiar with DOS command lines on Microsoft Windows, the Terminal is somewhat similar (but much more powerful).

Inside each Terminal window, there is a special program running called a *shell*. The shell does four simple things:

1. It *displays a prompt* in the Terminal window, waiting for you to type a command and press Enter.
2. It *reads your command* and interprets any special symbols you typed.
3. It *runs the command*, automatically locating any necessary programs.
4. It *prints the output*, if any, in the Terminal window.

The Terminal's job is merely to open windows and manage shells. Using the Terminal, you can resize the windows, change their colors and fonts, and perform copy and paste operations. But it's the shell that is doing the real work of reading and running commands. Figure 1-1 shows how the Terminal and the shell work together: when you peer into a Terminal window, you are viewing a shell, which in turn interacts with your Macintosh.

What's a Command?

OS X comes with over 1,000 commands for file manipulation, text editing, printing, mathematics, computer programming, typesetting, networking...you name it. A typical command is run in a shell by typing its *program name*, followed by *options* and *arguments*, like this:

```
wc -l myfile
```

The program name (wc, the "word count" program) refers to a program somewhere on your Mac that the shell will locate and run. Options, which usually begin with a dash, affect the behavior of the program. In the preceding command, the -l

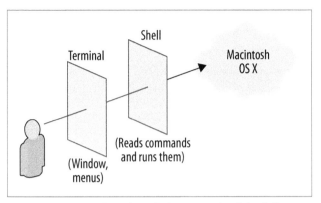

Figure 1-1. Viewing OS X through the Terminal and the shell

option tells **wc** to count lines and not words. The argument **myfile** specifies the file that **wc** should read and process.

Case Sensitivity

The commands in this book should be entered exactly, using the same capital (uppercase) and small (lowercase) letters we provide. In other words, commands are case-sensitive. If a command is **wc -l** (small "L") but you type **wc -L** (capital "L"), it will not work.

In some situations, capital and small letters are equivalent. Specifically, the names of files and folders are case-insensitive, so when they appear on a command line, you can use capital or small letters as you see fit. Nevertheless, the rest of the command line is case-sensitive, so we recommend not changing the case of any letters in the presented commands.

Commands can have multiple options and arguments. Options may be given individually:

    wc -l -w myfile   *Two individual options*

or combined behind a single dash:

    wc -lw myfile   *Same as -l -w*

though some programs are quirky and do not recognize combined options. Multiple arguments are also OK:

```
wc -l myfile1 myfile2        Count lines in two files
```

Options are not standardized. The same option letter (say, -l) may have different meanings to different programs: in wc -l it means "lines of text," but in ls -l it means "longer output." In the other direction, two programs might use different options to mean the same thing, such as -q for "run quietly" versus -s for "run silently."

Likewise, arguments are not standardized. They usually represent filenames for input or output, but they can be other things too, like directory names or regular expressions.

Commands can be more complex and interesting than a single program with options:

- Commands can run more than one program at a time, either in sequence (one program after another) or in a "pipeline" with the output of one command becoming the input of the next. Shell experts use pipelines all the time.

- Commands can run "in the background" while you do other work.

- The shell has a programming language built in. So instead of a command saying "run this program," it might say, "run this program six times" or "if today is Tuesday, run this program, otherwise run a different one."

The Command Prompt

Before you can type a command, you must wait for the shell to display a special symbol, called a *prompt*. A prompt means, "I am waiting for your next command." Prompts come in all shapes and sizes, depending how your shell is configured. Your prompt might be a dollar sign:

```
$
```

or a complex line of text containing your computer name, username, and possibly other information and symbols:

```
mymac:~smith$
```

or various other styles. All these prompts mean the same thing: the shell is ready for your commands.

In this book, we'll use the unique symbol ➜ to indicate a shell prompt, so you won't mistakenly type it as part of a command. Here is a prompt followed by a command:

```
➜ wc -l myfile
```

Some commands will print text on the screen as they run. To distinguish your command (which you type) from this printed output (which you don't), we'll display the command in bold like this:

```
➜ wc -l myfile          The command you type
  12  23 371 myfile      The output it produces
```

Some commands in this book can be run successfully only by an *administrator*, a special user with permission to do anything on the system. (Also called a *superuser* or *root*.) In this case, we precede the command with sudo, which we'll explain fully in "Becoming the Superuser" on page 145:

```
➜ sudo superuser command goes here
```

Ten Commands to Try

To give you a feel for the Terminal, here are 10 simple commands you can try right now. Open the Terminal by visiting your Mac's *Utilities* folder (in the Finder menu, choose Go and then Utilities), and double-click the Terminal icon. Then try these commands by typing them at the Terminal prompt. You must type them *exactly*, including capital and small letters, spaces, and all symbols.

Display a calendar for April, 2015:

```
→ cal apr 2015
      April 2015
Su Mo Tu We Th Fr Sa
          1  2  3  4
 5  6  7  8  9 10 11
12 13 14 15 16 17 18
19 20 21 22 23 24 25
26 27 28 29 30
```

List the contents of the *Applications* folder:

```
→ ls /Applications
Address Book.app  GarageBand.app      Mail.app
App Store.app     Image Capture.app   TextEdit.app
...
```

Count the number of items in your *Documents* folder:

```
→ ls $HOME/Documents | wc -l
67
```

See how much space is used on your internal hard disk:

```
→ df -h /
Filesystem     Size   Used  Avail Capacity  Mounted on
/dev/disk0s2   465Gi  98Gi  366Gi    22%     /
```

Watch the processes running on your Mac (type "q" to quit):

```
→ top
```

Print the file */etc/hosts* on your default printer, if you have one:

```
→ lpr /etc/hosts
```

See how long you've been logged in to your Mac:

```
→ last -1 $USER
smith  console    Wed Apr 25 10:45   still logged in
```

Download a PDF file from the Internet to your Mac desktop, without needing a web browser. This involves two commands, and the O is a capital letter, not a zero:

```
→ curl -O http://www.blazemonger.com/sample.pdf
→ mv sample.pdf $HOME/Desktop
```

Display the IP address of your Mac:

```
→ ipconfig getifaddr en0        For wired
→ ipconfig getifaddr en1        For wireless
192.168.1.47
```

See who owns the domain name **oreilly.com** (press the space bar to move forward page by page, and type "q" to quit):

```
→ whois oreilly.com | less
```

Finally, clear the window and exit Terminal:

```
→ clear
→ exit
```

OK, that was more than 10 commands...but congratulations: you are now a Terminal user! These commands are just quick examples; we will see more detailed and complex commands later in the book.

Reading This Book

You don't have to read this book from start to finish: much of it is a reference for daily work. A typical pattern might be:

1. Look in the Table of Contents to find a general topic (say, viewing files).

2. The section for that topic ("File Viewing" on page 54) begins with a list of relevant commands (**cat**, **tail**, etc.).

3. Read about the command you want (e.g., **tail**).

We'll describe many commands in this book. Each description begins with a standard heading about the command; Figure 1-2 shows one for the **ls** (list files) command. This heading demonstrates the general usage in a simple format:

```
ls [options] [files]
```

| ls | | stdin | **stdout** | -file | **--opt** | --help | --version |

```
ls [options] [files]
```

Figure 1-2. Standard command heading

which means you'd type "ls" followed, if you choose, by options and then filenames. You wouldn't type the square brackets "[" and "]": they just indicate their contents are optional; and words in italics mean you have to fill in your own specific values, like names of actual files. You may see a vertical bar between options or arguments, perhaps grouped by parentheses:

```
(file | directory)
```

This indicates choice: you may supply either a filename or directory name as an argument.

The standard heading in Figure 1-2 also lists six properties of the command printed in black (meaning the property is supported by the command) or gray (unsupported):

stdin

> This means the command reads from your keyboard, which goes by the name "standard input" (stdin).

stdout

> The command writes to your screen, which goes by the name "standard output" (stdout).

-file

> When given a dash (-) argument in place of an input filename, the command reads from standard input; and likewise, if the dash is supplied as an output filename, the command writes to standard output. For example, the following wc command line reads the files *file1* and *file2*, then standard input, then *file3*:

> ```
> → wc file1 file2 - file3
> ```

-- opt

> If you supply the command-line option "--" it means "end of options": anything appearing later on the command line is not an option. This is sometimes necessary to operate on a file whose name begins with a dash, which otherwise would be (mistakenly) treated as an option. For example, if you have a file named *-foo*, the command `wc -foo` will fail because `-foo` will be treated as an (invalid) option. `wc -- -foo` works. If a command does not support "--", you can prepend the symbols "./" to the filename so the dash is no longer the first character:

> → `wc ./-foo`

> This tells the shell that `-foo` is the name of a file in the current working directory and not an option.

--help

> The option `--help` makes the command print a help message explaining proper usage, then exit.

--version

> The option `--version` makes the command print its version information and exit.

Standard Input and Output

Many commands accept input and produce output. Input can come from your keyboard, which is given the fancy name *standard input*, or from files, or from other commands. Likewise, output is printed on screen (known as *standard output*), or written to files, or sent to other commands. Error messages are treated specially and displayed on *standard error*, which is usually also on screen but is kept separate from standard output.[1]

Later we'll see how to *redirect* standard input, output, and error to make commands communicate with files and with each other. But for now let's just make sure you know the vocabu-

---

1. For example, you can capture standard output in a file and still have standard error messages appear on screen.

lary. When we say a command "reads," we mean from standard input unless we say otherwise. And when a command "writes" or "prints," we mean on standard output, unless we're talking about computer printers.

Keystrokes

Throughout the book, we use certain symbols to indicate keystrokes. The ^ symbol means "press and hold the Control (Ctrl) key," so for example, ^D (pronounced "control D") means "press and hold the Control key and type D." The shell tends to employ the Control key as a modifier rather than the Mac's option or command (⌘) keys.

We also write ESC to mean "press the Escape key." Keys like Enter and space bar should be self-explanatory.

Long lines

If a shell command is too wide for this book, we break it onto multiple lines, and the symbol \ means "continued on the next line":

```
→ wc -l file_with_a_long_name another_long_file_name \
  yet_another_long_file_name
```

This slash isn't just a visual aid: it actually works in the shell. (It is known as a line-continuation character.) If you type one of these slashes, it must be the last character on its line: you must press Enter immediately after it.

Your friend, the echo command

In many of our examples, we'll print information to the screen with the echo command, which we'll formally describe in "Screen Output" on page 170. echo is one of the simplest commands: it merely prints its arguments on standard output, once those arguments have been processed by the shell:

```
→ echo My dog has fleas
My dog has fleas
→ echo My name is $USER          Shell variable USER
My name is smith
```

Quick help

If you need more information than is found in this book, type
man (short for "manual") followed by any command name:

➜ man wc

This runs the man command, which displays documentation
about a command one page at a time. This documentation is
called a *manpage* (i.e., "manual page"). Press the space bar to
see the next page of documentation, type b to go back to the
previous page, or type q to quit. To learn more about the man
command, run man man. More details are found in "Getting
Help" on page 209.

Now that you've seen how this book works, let's begin learning
about the Terminal and the shell.

Running the Terminal

The Terminal is simple to run. Visit your Mac's *Utilities* folder,
locate the Terminal icon, and launch it. A Terminal window
will appear, as in Figure 1-3, ready for your commands. If you
run Terminal often, place its icon into the application dock for
convenience.

If you're already running the Terminal, its Shell menu provides
several ways to work with shells, shown in Figure 1-4:

New Window (⌘N)
  Open a Terminal window running a shell.

New Tab (⌘T)
  In the current Terminal window, which is already running
  a shell, open another tab with its own shell. (Similar to the
  tabs in web browsers such as Firefox and Safari.)

New Command... (⇧⌘N)
  Run a single command in a shell, then terminate the shell.
  This feature opens a Terminal window and leaves it hang-
  ing around, useless, after the shell is finished. We don't
  see much point to this feature.

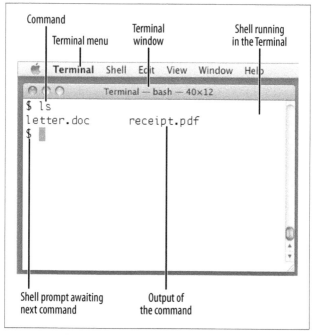

Figure 1-3. The Terminal application running a shell

Figure 1-4. The Shell menu in the Terminal

The Terminal is the standard method for running shells on the Mac desktop, but it's not the only way. You can also log in to a Macintosh remotely from another computer. We'll cover this advanced topic in "Running a Shell Remotely" on page 183.

The Filesystem

If you think Macintosh files are just little icons on your desktop, it's time to learn something new. When you access files from a command line rather than the Finder, things look pretty different.

Centuries ago, people believed that the Earth was the center of the solar system and everything revolved around it, even the sun. They believed this because they saw the sun move through the sky each day. But in reality, the sun is in the center, and Earth is merely one planet orbiting it.

The Macintosh desktop has a similar illusion. When you log in to the Mac, everything on the desktop seems to revolve around *you*: your files, your home folder, your trash, and your system preferences. It feels like you are in the center, surrounded by the rest of the Mac's files, folders, and features. In reality, however, your desktop isn't the center of anything: it's just one "planet" (really a folder) in a solar system of files and folders, called the *OS X filesystem*, or just "the filesystem."

In the following sections, we'll introduce you to the true filesystem as viewed through the Terminal. This view might seem like an alien world because your familiar files and folders won't have any icons, just words on a command line. Nevertheless, you *must become comfortable* with this view to take advantage of the Terminal's powerful features. For some people, this is the most challenging aspect of getting started with the Terminal and shell.

Structure of the Filesystem

The OS X filesystem is a hierarchy, or *tree*, of folders and files, as in Figure 1-5. At the top is a folder called the *root directory*. Below the root are several folders you might recognize, like *Applications*, and others that might be less familiar, like *bin* and *etc*. These folders-within-a-folder are called *subdirec-*

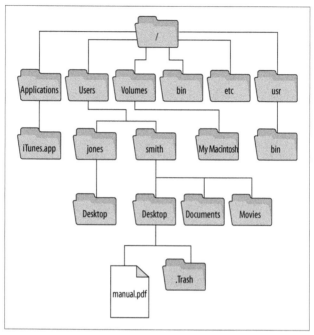

Figure 1-5. The OS X filesystem (partial). The root directory is at the top. The PDF file's full path is /Users/smith/Desktop/manual.pdf

tories. Each subdirectory may itself contain other files and subdirectories, and so on, into infinity.

This filesystem view is not the same one you see in Finder windows. The Finder hides some folders from you, such as *etc*, because they contain operating system files that most users don't need to access. It also displays disks and certain folders more prominently, such as *Applications*, by listing them on the left-hand side of Finder windows. This is just the user-friendly illusion of the desktop. The filesystem tree in Figure 1-5 is the reality.

Folders and Directories

The words "folder" and "directory" are synonyms: they both
mean a container for files (and other folders) on your Mac.
When using the Finder, people almost always say "folder," but
when using a command line (as in the Terminal and shell), the
word "directory" is more common. In this book, we use the
terms "directory" and "subdirectory" often.

Each file and directory has a unique name in the filesystem,
called a *path*, written with words and slashes. The root
directory's path is a slash (/). Below the root, the Applications
subdirectory has the path */Applications*, and below it, the
subdirectory iTunes.app has the path */Applications/
iTunes.app*. In general, a path like:

    /one/two/three/four

says that the root directory contains a directory called *one*,
which contains a directory *two*, which contains a directory
three, which contains a final file or directory, *four*.

Figure 1-5 reveals the truth behind your desktop in the OS X
"solar system." If your username is smith, then all the files and
folders you see displayed on your desktop live inside the
folder */Users/smith/Desktop*. So when you see a PDF file on
your desktop, *manual.pdf*, its true path in the OS X filesystem
is */Users/smith/Desktop/manual.pdf*. Now the illusion of the
desktop is fully revealed: your "central," graphical desktop is
actually three levels deep in the OS X filesystem, and no more
special than any other user's *Desktop* folder. Figure 1-6 reveals
the true filesystem location of other common parts of the desktop: the system disk, the trash, and more.

Navigating the Filesystem

When you open a Finder window and work with its icons, that
window represents a particular folder. Likewise, when you
open a Terminal window, its shell is working "in" some direc-

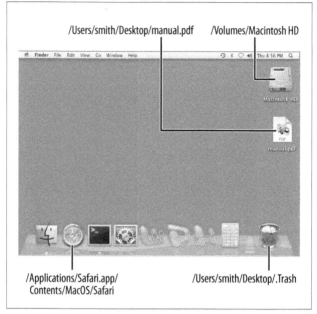

/Users/smith/Desktop/manual.pdf   /Volumes/Macintosh HD

/Applications/Safari.app/   /Users/smith/Desktop/.Trash
Contents/MacOS/Safari

Figure 1-6. Behind the desktop illusion: some icons and their true filesystem paths

tory. More technically, your shell has a *current working directory* (analogous to your open Finder window). When you run commands in that shell, they operate relative to the current working directory. Figure 1-7 illustrates this concept. If your shell is "in" the directory */Users/smith/stuff*, and you run a command that refers to a file *receipt.pdf*, then the file is really */Users/smith/stuff/receipt.pdf*.

If a path begins with a slash, such as */one/two/three*, it's called an *absolute* path. If not, it's a *relative* path, because it's relative to a shell's current location in the filesystem. For instance, a relative path *a/b/c*, when referenced from the current directory */one/two/three*, implies the absolute path */one/two/three/a/b/c*. In general, if you refer to a relative file path in a shell, the path is relative to your current working directory.

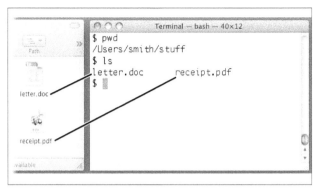

Figure 1-7. A Finder window (left) and Terminal window (right) displaying the same folder, /Users/smith/stuff

Two special relative paths are . (a single period) and .. (two periods in a row). A single period refers to your current directory, and two periods means your *parent* directory, one level above. So if your current directory is */one/two/three*, then . refers to this directory and .. refers to */one/two*. This explains what we did in "Reading This Book" on page 9, when we wrote ./-foo to indicate that -foo was a file in the current directory, and not an option.

You "move" your shell from one directory to another using the cd ("change directory") command:

→ **cd /one/two/three**

More technically, the cd command changes your shell's current working directory, in this case to */one/two/three*. This is an absolute change (since the directory begins with "/"); of course you can make relative moves as well:

| → **cd d** | *Enter subdirectory d* |
| → **cd ../mydir** | *Go up to my parent, then into directory mydir* |

While you're cd-ing around the filesystem, you must remember which directory you're "in." If you need a reminder, run the pwd command to print the name of your current working directory:

```
→ pwd
/Users/smith/stuff
```

File and directory names may contain most characters you expect: letters,[2] digits, periods, dashes, underscores, and most symbols (but not "/", which is reserved for separating directories). For practical use, however, don't create names with spaces, asterisks, question marks, parentheses, and other characters that have special meaning to the shell. Otherwise, you'll need to quote or escape these characters all the time. (See "Quoting" on page 34.)

Home Directories in the Filesystem

Users' personal files are found in the */Users* directory. Each user has a subdirectory named */Users/your-username*: take for example, */Users/smith* or */Users/jones*. This is called your *home directory*. OS X provides several ways to locate or refer to your home directory:

In the Finder

On the left side of a Finder window, you may see an icon labeled with your username (e.g., "Smith"). This represents the home directory */Users/smith*. Click it to access your home directory via the Finder. If you don't see this icon, you can add it: visit the Finder menu, choose Preferences, click Sidebar, and add the icon.

cd

With no arguments, the **cd** command returns you (i.e., sets the shell's working directory) to your home directory:

HOME *variable*

The environment variable HOME (see "Shell variables" on page 29) contains the name of your home directory.

---

2. OS X filenames are case-insensitive, so capital (uppercase) and small (lowercase) letters are equivalent. (This can be changed if you are technically inclined.) Commands, however, are case-sensitive.

```
→ echo $HOME          The echo command prints its arguments
/Users/smith
```

~

When used in place of a directory, a lone tilde is expanded by the shell to the name of your home directory.

```
→ echo ~
/Users/smith
```

When followed by a username (as in ~*fred*), the shell expands this string to be the user's home directory:

```
→ cd ~fred
→ pwd                 The "print working directory" command
/Users/fred
```

System Directories in the Filesystem

A typical Macintosh has thousands of system directories. These directories contain operating system files, applications, documentation, and just about everything *except* personal user files (which typically live in your home directory).

Unless you're a system administrator, you'll rarely visit most system directories—but with a little knowledge you can understand or guess their purposes. Their names often contain three parts, which we'll call the scope, category, and application. (These are not standard terms, but they'll help you understand things.) For example, the directory */usr/local/share/emacs*, which contains local data for the Emacs text editor, has scope */usr/local* (locally installed system files), category *share* (program-specific data and documentation), and application Emacs (a text editor), shown in Figure 1-8. We'll explain these three parts, slightly out of order.

Figure 1-8. Directory scope, category, and application

Directory path part 1: category

A *category* tells you the types of files found in a directory. For example, if the category is *bin*, you can be reasonably assured that the directory contains programs. Common categories are:

Categories for programs

Applications	Macintosh applications
bin	Command-line programs, usually binary files
sbin	Command-line programs intended to be run by the superuser
lib	Libraries of code used by programs
libexec	Programs invoked by other programs, not usually by users; think "library of executable programs"

Categories for documentation

doc	Documentation
info	Documentation files for Emacs's built-in help system
man	Documentation files (manual pages) displayed by the man program; the files are often compressed, or sprinkled with typesetting commands for man to interpret
share	Program-specific files, such as examples and installation instructions

Categories for configuration

etc	Configuration files for the system (and other miscellaneous stuff)
Library	Files that support Macintosh applications

Categories for programming

include	Header files for programming
src	Source code for programs

Categories for web files

cgi-bin	Scripts/programs that run on web pages
html	Web pages
public_html	Web pages, typically in users' home directories
www	Web pages

Categories for display

| *fonts* | Fonts (surprise!) |
| *X11* | X Window System files |

Categories for hardware

| *dev* | Device files for interfacing with disks and other hardware |

Categories for runtime files

var	Files specific to this computer, created and updated as the computer runs
log	Log files that track important system events, containing error, warning, and informational messages
mail	Mailboxes for incoming mail
run	PID files, which contain the IDs of running processes; these files are often consulted to track or kill particular processes
spool	Files queued or in transit, such as outgoing email, print jobs, and scheduled jobs
tmp	Temporary storage for programs and/or people to use

Directory path part 2: scope

The *scope* of a directory path describes, at a high level, the purpose of an entire directory hierarchy. Some common ones are:

/	(Pronounced "root.") The most fundamental system files supplied with OS X
/private	System configuration files hidden from the Finder
/usr	More system files supplied with OS X (pronounced "user")
/usr/local	System files not supplied with OS X and installed by you (or another administrator)
/usr/X11	Files pertaining to the X Window System
/Volumes	Access to all disks connected to the Macintosh.

Directory path part 3: application

The application part of a directory path, if present, is usually the name of a program. After the scope and category (say, */usr/local/doc*), a program may have its own subdirectory (say, */usr/local/doc/myprogram*) containing files it needs.

File Protections

A Macintosh may have many users with login accounts. To maintain privacy and security, most users can access only *some* files on the system, not all. This access control is embodied in two questions:

Who has permission?

> Every file and directory has an *owner* who has permission to do anything with it. Typically the user who created a file is its owner, but relationships can be more complex.
>
> Additionally, a predefined *group* of users may have permission to access a file. Groups are defined by the system administrator and are covered in "Group Management" on page 147.
>
> Finally, a file or directory can be opened to *all users* with login accounts on the system. You'll also see this set of users called *the world* or simply *other*.

What kind of permission is granted?

> File owners, groups, and the world may each have permission to *read*, *write* (modify), and *execute* (run) particular files. Permissions also extend to directories, which users may read (access files within the directory), write (create and delete files within the directory), and execute (enter the directory with cd).

To see the ownership and permissions of a file, run the ls -l command, described in more detail in "Basic File Operations" on page 45:

```
→ ls -l myfile
-rw-r--r-- 1 smith staff   7384 Jan 04 22:40 myfile
```

In the output, the file permissions are the 10 leftmost characters:

```
-rw-r--r--
```

a string of r (read), w (write), x (execute), dashes, and sometimes other letters and symbols. Reading from left to right (positions 1–10), the permissions mean:

Position	Meaning
1	File type. A dash (-) means a plain file and d means a directory. Other more advanced values include l (symbolic link), p (named pipe), c (character device), and b (block device).
2–4	Owner permissions: read, write, and execute permissions for the file's owner.
5–7	Group permissions: read, write, and execute permissions for the file's group.
8–10	World permissions: read, write, and execute permissions for all other users.

So in our example, the permissions -rw-r--r-- mean that the file *myfile* can be read and written by the owner (smith), read by members of the staff group, and read by the rest of the world.

To see the ownership and permissions of a directory, add the -d option to the earlier ls command (otherwise you'll list the directory's contents):

```
→ ls -ld dirname
drwxr-x--- 3 smith staff   4096 Jan 08 15:02 dirname
```

The permissions drwxr-x--- indicate that the directory *dirname* can be read, written, and entered (execute permission) by the owner smith, read or entered by anyone in the staff group, and not accessed at all by any other users.

To change the owner, group ownership, or permissions of a file, use the chown, chgrp, and chmod commands, respectively, as described in "File Properties" on page 68.

The Shell

In order to use commands on a Macintosh, you'll need a program that reads and executes them. That program is called the *shell*, which runs inside the Terminal and is OS X's command-line user interface.[3] You type a command and press Enter, and the shell runs whatever program (or programs) you've requested. For example, to list the files in your *Documents* folder, one per line, you could execute the `ls -1` command in a shell:

```
→ ls -1 ~/Documents
data.pdf
letter.txt
song.mp3
```

A single command can also invoke several programs at the same time, and even connect programs together so they interact. Here's a command that redirects the output of the preceding `ls` command to become the input of the `wc` program, which counts lines of text in a file; the result is the number of lines printed by `ls`:

```
→ ls -1 ~/Documents | wc -1
3
```

telling you how many files are in your *Documents* folder. The vertical bar, called a *pipe*, makes the connection between `ls` and `wc`.

A shell is actually a program itself, and OS X has several different ones: the Bourne shell, the Korn shell, the C shell, and others. This book focuses on a popular shell called bash, the Bourne-Again Shell, located in */bin/bash*, which is the default for user accounts. However, all these shells have similar basic functions.

The Shell Versus Programs

When you run a command, it might invoke an OS X program (like `ls`), or instead it might be a *built-in command*, a feature of the shell itself. You can tell the difference with the `type` command:

```
→ type ls
ls is /bin/ls
→ type cd
cd is a shell builtin
```

---

3. The same shell is found on Linux systems, and on Windows PCs that run Cygwin.

The next few sections describe built-in features of the shell.

Selected Features of the bash Shell

A shell does much more than simply run commands. It also has powerful features to make this task easier: wildcards for matching filenames, a "command history" to recall previous commands quickly, pipes for making the output of one command become the input of another, variables for storing values for use by the shell, and more. Take the time to learn these features, and you will become faster and more productive. Let's skim the surface and introduce you to these useful tools. (For full documentation, run info bash.)

Wildcards

Wildcards are a shorthand for sets of files with similar names. For example, a* means all files whose names begin with lowercase "a." Wildcards are "expanded" by the shell into the actual set of filenames they match. So if you type:

   → ls a*

the shell first expands a* into the filenames that begin with "a" in your current directory, as if you had typed:

   → ls aardvark adamantium apple

ls never knows you used a wildcard: it sees only the final list of filenames after the shell expands the wildcard. Importantly, this means *every* command, regardless of its origin, works with wildcards and other shell features.

Here's an example of wildcard use. Suppose you have a folder containing hundreds of JPEG images from your digital camera, named *IMG_1001.jpg* through *IMG_1864.jpg*. You need to delete all the images ending in *20.jpg*:

```
IMG_1020.jpg
IMG_1120.jpg
IMG_1220.jpg
IMG_1320.jpg ...
```

The names of these files are not consecutive, nor are their dates, so you have no easy way to select these files as a group in the Finder and drag them to the trash. Using a shell wildcard, you can list them with a single `ls` command:

→ `ls *20.jpg`

and delete them with a single `rm` command, which removes files:

→ `rm *20.jpg`   *Careful! Deletes files immediately!*

There are two characters that wildcards cannot match: a leading period, and the directory slash (/). These must be given literally, as in `.pro*` to match *.profile*, or `/etc/*conf` to match all filenames ending in *conf* in the */etc* directory.

Dot Files

Filenames with a leading period, called *dot files*, are special in OS X. When you name a file beginning with a period:

- `ls` omits the file from directory listings, unless you provide the `-a` option.
- Shell wildcards do not match the leading period.

Effectively, dot files are hidden unless you explicitly ask to see them. As a result, sometimes they are called "hidden files."

Wildcard	Meaning
*	Zero or more consecutive characters.
?	A single character.
[set]	Any single character in the given *set*, most commonly a sequence of characters, like [aeiouAEIOU] for all vowels, or a range with a dash, like [A-Z] for all capital letters.
[^set]	Any single character *not* in the given *set*. For example, [^A-Z] means any single character that is not a capital letter.
[!set]	! is equivalent to ^.

When using character sets, if you want to include a literal dash in the set, put it first or last. To include a literal closing square bracket in the set, put it first. To include a ^ or ! symbol literally, don't put it first.

Brace expansion

Similar to wildcards, expressions with curly braces also expand to become multiple arguments to a command. The comma-separated expression:

```
{X,YY,ZZZ}
```

expands first to X, then YY, and finally ZZZ within a command line, like this:

```
→ echo sand{X,YY,ZZZ}wich
sandXwich sandYYwich sandZZZwich
```

Braces work with any strings, unlike wildcards, which are limited to filenames. The preceding example works regardless of which files are in the current directory.

Shell variables

You can define variables and their values by assigning them:

```
→ MYVAR=3
```

To produce the value of a variable, simply place a dollar sign in front of the variable name:

```
→ echo $MYVAR
3
```

Some variables are standard and commonly defined by your shell upon login.

Variable	Meaning
DISPLAY	The name of your display for opening X Windows
HOME	Your home directory, such as /Users/smith
LOGNAME	Your login name, such as smith
MAIL	Your incoming mailbox, such as /var/spool/mail/smith
OLDPWD	Your shell's previous directory, prior to the last cd command

Variable	Meaning
PATH	Your shell search path: directories separated by colons
PWD	Your shell's current directory
SHELL	The path to your shell, e.g., */bin/bash*
TERM	The type of your terminal, e.g., xterm or vt100
USER	Your login name

To see a shell's variables, run:

```
→ printenv            All variables and their values
→ printenv HOME       One variable and its value
→ echo $HOME          One variable and its value
```

The scope of the variable (i.e., which programs know about it) is, by default, the shell in which it's defined. To make a variable and its value available to other programs your shell invokes (i.e., subshells), use the **export** command:

```
→ export MYVAR
```

or the shorthand to export and assign in one step:

```
→ export MYVAR=3
```

Your variable is now called an *environment variable*, since it's available to other programs in your shell's "environment." So in the preceding example, the exported variable MYVAR is available to all programs run by that same shell (including shell scripts: see "Variables" on page 197).

To make a variable value available to a specific program just once, prepend *variable=value* to the command line:

```
→ printenv HOME
/Users/smith
→ HOME=/Users/sally  printenv HOME
/Users/sally
→ printenv HOME
/Users/smith                    The original value is unaffected
```

Search path

Programs are scattered all over the filesystem, in directories like */bin* and */usr/bin*. When you run a program via a shell command, how does the shell find it? The critical variable PATH tells the shell where to look. When you type any command:

```
→ ls
```

the shell has to find the ls program by searching through directories. The shell consults the value of PATH, which is a sequence of directories separated by colons:

```
→ echo $PATH
/usr/local/bin:/bin:/usr/bin:/Users/smith/bin
```

and looks for the ls command in each of these directories. If it finds ls (say, */bin/ls*), it runs the command. Otherwise, it reports:

```
-bash: ls: command not found
```

To add directories to your shell's search path temporarily, modify its PATH variable. For example, to append */usr/sbin* to your shell's search path, run:

```
→ PATH=$PATH:/usr/sbin
```

Now the additional directory is in the search path:

```
→ echo $PATH
/usr/local/bin:/bin:/usr/bin:/Users/smith/bin:/usr/sbin
```

This change affects only the current shell. To make it permanent, put the same PATH command into your startup file *$HOME/.bash_profile*, as explained in "Tailoring Shell Behavior" on page 43. Then close your Terminal window and open a new one for the change to take effect.

Aliases

The built-in command **alias** defines a convenient shorthand for a longer command, to save typing. For example:

```
→ alias ll='ls -l'
```

defines a new command ll that runs ls -l:

```
→ ll
total 436
-rw-r--r--    1 smith       3584 Oct 11 14:59 file1
-rwxr-xr-x    1 smith         72 Aug  6 23:04 file2
...
```

To remove an alias, use the **unalias** command:

```
→ unalias ll
```

Define aliases in your *$HOME/.bash_profile* file (see "Tailoring Shell Behavior" on page 43) to make them available whenever you run a shell. To list all your aliases, type **alias**. If aliases don't seem powerful enough for you (since they carry no parameters or branching), see "Programming with Shell Scripts" on page 194, or run **info bash** and read up on "shell functions."

Input/output redirection

The shell can redirect standard input, standard output, and standard error to and from files. (We introduced these terms in "Standard Input and Output" on page 11.) In other words, any command that reads from standard input can read from a file instead with the shell's < operator:

```
→ some command < infile
```

Likewise, any command that writes to standard output can write to a file instead:

→ *some command* > **outfile**	*Create/overwrite outfile*
→ *some command* >> **outfile**	*Append to outfile*

A command that writes to standard error can have its output redirected to a file as well, using the 2> operator, while standard output still goes to the screen:

→ *some command* 2> **errorfile**	*Create/overwrite outfile*

To redirect both standard output and standard error to files, you can supply both > and 2> to redirect them to separate files, or >& to redirect them both to the same file:

```
→ some command > outfile 2> errorfile     Separate files
→ some command >& outfile                  Single file
```

Be careful: when you redirect output to a file, the file gets over-written without any warning, unless you are appending with the >> operator.

Pipes

You can redirect the standard output of one command to be the standard input of another, using the shell's pipe (|) oper-ator. For example, this command sends the output of **ls** (list files) into the **wc** (word count) program:

```
→ ls | wc -l
```

which prints a count of files in the current directory. Multiple pipes work, too: let's build a four-stage pipeline one step at a time. First, we list files in the current directory:

```
→ ls -1
data.pdf
letter.txt
song.mp3
symphony.mp3
...
```

Then we extract the file extensions with the **cut** command (de-scribed in "File Text Manipulation" on page 81), which re-moves columns of text:

```
→ ls -1 | cut -d. -f2
pdf
txt
mp3
mp3
...
```

Then we sort the results with the **sort** command (also in "File Text Manipulation" on page 81):

```
→ ls -1 | cut -d. -f2 | sort
mp3
mp3
pdf
txt
...
```

Finally, in case the output is long, we pipe it through the `less` command (found in "File Viewing" on page 54) that pauses the output whenever the shell window fills up:

```
→ ls -1 | cut -d. -f2 | sort | less
```

Pipes are one of the most powerful, useful, and downright fun features of the shell.

Combining commands

You can run several commands in sequence on a single command line. There are three ways to do this with different behavior. If you separate the commands with semicolons, they run as if you'd entered them separately at individual shell prompts:

```
→ command1 ; command2 ; command3
```

If any of the commands fail, the sequence continues. In contrast, if you separate the commands with `&&` symbols (pronounced "and"), the sequence will stop if any command fails:

```
→ command1 && command2 && command3
```

Finally, if you separate the commands with `||` symbols (pronounced "or"), the sequence will stop as soon as one command succeeds:

```
→ command1 || command2 || command3
```

Quoting

Normally, words on the command line are separated by spaces, tabs, or linebreaks (collectively called *whitespace*). If you want a word to *contain* whitespace (e.g., a filename with a space in it), surround it with single or double quotes to make the shell treat it as a unit. For example, the filename `My Stuff` would need to be quoted or else the shell will think you mean two files named `My` and `Stuff`:

```
→ wc My Stuff                          Wrong
wc: My: open: No such file or directory
wc: Stuff: open: No such file or directory
```

```
→ wc "My Stuff"                          Correct
10      34      236 My Stuff
```

Single quotes treat their contents literally, while double quotes let shell constructs be evaluated, such as variables:

```
→ echo 'The variable HOME has value $HOME'
The variable HOME has value $HOME
→ echo "The variable HOME has value $HOME"
The variable HOME has value /Users/smith
```

Backquotes ("backticks") are the coolest quotes. They cause their contents to be evaluated as a shell command. The contents are then replaced by the standard output of the command:

```
→ whoami                    Program that prints your username
smith
→ echo My name is `whoami`
My name is smith
```

Escaping

If a character has special meaning to the shell but you want it used literally (e.g., treating * as a literal asterisk rather than a wildcard), precede the character with the backward slash "\" character. This is called *escaping* the special character:

```
→ echo a*                   The wildcard matches "a" filenames
aardvark  agnostic  apple
→ echo a\*                  A literal asterisk
a*
→ echo "I live in $HOME"    Dollar sign means a variable value
I live in /Users/smith
→ echo "I live in \$HOME"   A literal dollar sign
I live in $HOME
```

You can also escape control characters (tabs, newlines, ^D, and so forth) to have them used literally on the command line, if you precede them with ^V. This is particularly useful for tab (^I) characters, which the shell would otherwise use for filename completion (see "Filename completion" on page 38):

```
→ echo "There is a tab between here^V^I and here"
There is a tab between here        and here
```

Command-line editing

Bash lets you edit the command line you're working on using cursor movement keys. If you like the text editors Emacs and vim (see "File Creation and Editing" on page 63), you can also use their keystrokes for editing the command line. Emacs keystrokes work by default. To enable command-line editing with vim keys, run this command (and place it in your *$HOME/.bash_profile* to make it permanent):

→ `set -o vi`

To re-enable Emacs keystrokes, run:

→ `set -o emacs`

Here are some useful keystrokes; see "File Creation and Editing" on page 63 for others:

Operation	Cursor keys	Emacs keystroke	vim keystroke (after ESC)
Go forward one character	Right arrow	^F	l
Go backward one character	Left arrow	^B	h
Go forward one word	Ctrl + right arrow	ALT-f	w
Go backward one word	Ctrl + left arrow	ALT-b	b
Delete forward one word		ALT-d	de
Delete backward one word		^W	db
Go to beginning of line	Home	^A	0
Go to end of line	End	^E	$
Delete next character	Delete	^D	x

Operation	Cursor keys	Emacs keystroke	vim keystroke (after ESC)
Erase everything from your cursor back to the shell prompt		^U	^U

Command history

You can recall previous commands you've run—that is, the shell's *history*—and re-execute them. Some useful history-related commands are listed below.

Command	Meaning
`history`	Print your history
`history` *N*	Print the most recent *N* commands in your history
`history -c`	Clear (delete) your history
`!!`	Re-run previous command
`!`*N*	Re-run command number *N* in your history
`!-`*N*	Re-run the command you typed *N* commands ago

`!$`	Represents the last parameter from the previous command; great for checking that files are present before removing them:
	
	`→ ls a*`
	`acorn.txt    affidavit`
	`→ rm !$` *Note: This deletes files!*

`!*`	Represents all parameters from the previous command:
	
	`→ ls a b c`
	`a    b    c`
	`→ wc !*`
	`   103    252   2904 a`
	`    12     25    384 b`
	`  25473  65510 988215 c`
	`  25588  65787 991503 total`

There are also keystrokes for searching the command history interactively, using cursor keys or Emacs/vim keystrokes:

Operation	Cursor keys	Emacs keystroke	vim keystroke (after ESC)
Go to previous command	Up arrow	^P	k
Go to next command	Down arrow	^N	j
Interactive search mode		^R	^R

Interactive search mode is extremely useful. Type ^R, then type any part of a previous command and see what appears. To continue jumping backward in history, type ^R additional times. When you see the command you want, press Enter to run it (or use other keystrokes to edit it). To cancel the search, type ^C.

Filename completion

Press the Tab key while you are in the middle of typing a filename, and the shell will automatically complete (finish typing) the filename for you. If several filenames match what you've typed so far, the shell will beep, indicating the match is ambiguous. Immediately press Tab again and the shell will present the alternatives. Try this:

```
→ cd /usr/bin
→ ls un TAB TAB
```

The shell will display all files in /usr/bin that begin with un, such as uniq, units, and unzip. Type a few more characters to disambiguate your choice some more, and press Tab again.

Shell Job Control

jobs	List your jobs.
&	Run a job in the background.
^Z	Suspend the current (foreground) job.
suspend	Suspend a shell.

| fg | Unsuspend a job: bring it into the foreground. |
| bg | Make a suspended job run in the background. |

All shells have *job control*: the ability to run programs in the background (multitasking behind the scenes) and foreground (running as the active process at your shell prompt). A *job* is simply the shell's unit of work. When you run a command interactively, your current shell tracks it as a job. When the command completes, the associated job disappears. Jobs are at a higher level than OS X processes (discussed in "Viewing Processes" on page 122); OS X knows nothing about them. They are merely constructs of the shell. Some important vocabulary about job control is:

Foreground job
> Running in a shell, occupying the shell prompt so you cannot run another command

Background job
> Running in a shell, but not occupying the shell prompt, so you can run another command in the same shell

Suspend
> To stop a foreground job temporarily

Resume
> To cause a suspended job to start running again

jobs

The built-in command jobs lists the jobs running in your current shell:

```
→ jobs
[1]-  Running              emacs myfile &
[2]+  Stopped              wc -l bigfile
```

The integer on the left is the job number, and the plus sign identifies the default job affected by the fg (foreground) and bg (background) commands.

&

Placed at the end of a command line, the ampersand causes the given command to run as a background job:

```
→ emacs myfile &
[2] 28090
```

The shell's response includes the job number (2) and the process ID of the command (28090).

^Z

Typing ^Z in a shell, while a job is running in the foreground, will suspend that job. It simply stops running, but its state is remembered:

```
→ sleep 20       Command that simply waits 20 seconds
^Z
[1]+  Stopped                 sleep 20
→
```

Now you're ready to type bg to put the command into the background where it continues running, or fg to resume it in the foreground.

bg

```
bg [%jobnumber]
```

The built-in command bg sends a suspended job to run in the background. With no arguments, bg operates on the most recently suspended job. To specify a particular job (shown by the jobs command), supply the job number preceded by a percent sign:

```
→ bg %2
```

Some types of interactive jobs cannot remain in the background—for instance, if they are waiting for input. If you try, the shell will suspend the job and display:

```
[2]+  Stopped                 command line here
```

You can now resume the job (with fg) and continue.

fg

`fg [%jobnumber]`

The built-in command **fg** brings a suspended or backgrounded job into the foreground. With no arguments, it selects a job, usually the most recently suspended or backgrounded one. To specify a particular job (as shown by the **jobs** command), supply the job number preceded by a percent sign:

   → **fg %2**

A typical sequence of job control commands is:

```
→ wc -l huge_file            Start a long job
^Z                           Suspend the job
[1]+  Stopped  wc -l huge_file
→ bg                         Put wc into the background
[1]+ wc -l huge_file &
→                            Run other commands...
→ fg                           Bring wc into the foreground
wc -l huge_file
578394783 huge_file              The wc job finishes
```

Start a long job and _Suspend the job_ and _Put wc into the background_ and _Run other commands..._ and _Bring wc into the foreground_ and _The wc job finishes_

---

suspend

The built-in command **suspend** will suspend the current shell if possible, as if you'd typed ^Z to the shell itself. For instance, if you've run the **sudo** command to make an administrator shell (see "Becoming the Superuser" on page 145) and want to return to your original shell:

```
→ whoami
smith
→ sudo bash
Password: *******
# whoami                  "#" is the superuser prompt
root
# suspend
[1]+  Stopped             sudo bash
→ whoami
smith
```

Killing a Command in Progress

If you've launched a command from the shell running in the foreground, and want to kill it immediately, type ^C. The shell recognizes ^C as meaning, "terminate the current foreground command right now." So if you are displaying a very long file (say, with the cat command) and want to stop, type ^C:

```
→ cat bigfile
This is a very long file with many lines. Blah blah blah
blah blah blah blahblahblah ^C
→
```

To kill a program running in the background, you can bring it into the foreground with fg and then type ^C. Alternatively, you can use the kill command (for more information, see "Controlling Processes" on page 126).

Killing a program is not a friendly way to end it. If the program has its own way to exit, use that when possible: see the sidebar for details.

Surviving a Kill

Killing a foreground program with ^C may leave your shell in an odd or unresponsive state, perhaps not displaying the keystrokes you type. This happens because the killed program had no opportunity to clean up after itself. If this happens to you:

1. Press ^J to get a shell prompt. This produces the same character as the Enter key (a newline) but will work even if Enter does not.

2. Type the shell command reset (even if the letters don't appear while you type) and press ^J again to run this command. This should bring your shell back to normal.

---

^C works only within shells. It will likely have no effect if typed in a window that is not a shell window. Additionally, some programs are written to "catch" the ^C and ignore it: an example is the text editor Emacs.

Terminating a Shell

To terminate a shell, run the **exit** command or type ^D.[4]

→ **exit**

or if you're running a Terminal window, click the close box.

Tailoring Shell Behavior

To configure all your shells to work in a particular way, edit the file *.bash_profile* in your home directory. This file executes each time you open bash in Terminal or log in remotely (discussed in "Running a Shell Remotely" on page 183). It can set variables and aliases, run programs, print your horoscope, or whatever you like.

This file is an example of a *shell script*: a file containing shell commands that can be executed as a unit. We'll cover this feature in more detail in "Programming with Shell Scripts" on page 194.

---

4. Control-D sends an "end of file" signal to any program reading from standard input. In this case, the program is the shell itself, which terminates.

CHAPTER 2

Commands

Now that you've seen an overview of the Terminal, the shell, and the Macintosh filesystem, we turn our attention to the *commands* you can run in the Terminal. We will list and describe the most useful commands for working with files, processes, users, networking, and more.

Basic File Operations

ls   List files in a directory.

cp   Copy a file.

mv   Rename ("move") a file.

rm   Delete ("remove") a file.

ln   Create links (alternative names) to a file.

One of the first things you'll want to do in Terminal is manipulate files: copying, renaming, deleting, and so forth.

ls   stdin   **stdout**   - file   **-- opt**   --help   --version

ls [*options*] [*files*]

The ls command (pronounced as it is spelled, *ell ess*) lists attributes of files and directories. You can list files in the current directory:

```
→ ls
```

in given directories:

```
→ ls dir1 dir2 dir3
```

or individually:

```
→ ls file1 file2 dir3/file3
```

The most important options are -a, -l, and -d. By default, ls hides files whose names begin with a dot, as explained in the sidebar "Dot Files" on page 28. The -a option displays all files:

```
→ ls
myfile1    myfile2
→ ls -a
.hidden_file    myfile1    myfile2
```

The -l option produces a long listing:

```
→ ls -l my.data
-rw-r--r--    1 smith users         149 Oct 28  2011 my.data
```

that includes, from left to right: the file's permissions (-rw-r--r--), owner (smith), group (users), size (149 bytes), last modification date (Oct 28 2011) and name. See "File Protections" on page 24 for more information on permissions.

Add the -@ option to -l to display OS X extended attributes of the files in question:

```
→ ls -l@ letter.docx
-rw-r--r--@  1 smith users    49269 Nov 19 2011 letter.docx
        com.apple.FinderInfo      32
```

The -d option lists information about a directory itself, rather than descending into the directory to list its files.

```
→ ls -ld my.dir
drwxr-xr-x    1 smith users        4096 Oct 29  2011 my.dir
```

Useful options

- -a   List all files, including those whose names begin with a dot.

- -l   Long listing, including file attributes. Add the -h option (human-readable) to print file sizes in kilobytes, megabytes, and gigabytes, instead of bytes.

- -@   Also display OS X extended attributes. (Combine with -l.)

- -F Decorate certain filenames with meaningful symbols, indicating their types. Appends "/" to directories, "*" to executables, "@" to symbolic links, "|" to named pipes, and "=" to sockets. These are just visual indicators for you, not part of the filenames!

- -i Prepend the inode numbers of the files.

- -s Prepend the size of the file in blocks, useful for sorting files by their size:

      → `ls -s | sort -n`

- -R If listing a directory, list its contents recursively.

- -d If listing a directory, do not list its contents, just the directory itself.

---

cp stdin   stdout   - file   -- **opt**   --help   --version

`cp [options] file1 file2`

`cp [options] (files | directories) directory`

The cp command normally copies a file:

   → `cp file file2`

or copies multiple files and directories into a destination directory:

   → `cp file1 file2 file3 dir4 destination_directory`

Using the -a option, you can also recursively copy directories.

Useful options

- -p Copy not only the file contents, but also the file's permissions, timestamps, and, if you have sufficient permission to do so, its owner and group. (Normally the copies will be owned by you, timestamped now, with permissions set by applying your umask to the original permissions.)

- -a Copy a directory hierarchy recursively, preserving all file attributes and links.

- -R Copy a directory hierarchy recursively. This option does not preserve the files' attributes such as permissions and timestamps. It does preserve symbolic links.

- -i Interactive mode. Ask before overwriting destination files.

- -f Force the copy. If a destination file exists, overwrite it unconditionally.

mv [*options*] *source target*

The mv (move) command can rename a file or directory:

> → mv file1 file2

or move files and directories into a destination directory:

> → mv file1 file2 dir3 dir4 *destination_directory*

Useful options

- -i   Interactive mode. Ask before overwriting destination files.

- -f   Force the move. If a destination file exists, overwrite it unconditionally.

---

rm [*options*] *files* | *directories*

The rm (remove) command can delete files:

> → rm file1 file2 file3

or recursively delete directories and all their subdirectories:

> → rm -r dir1 dir2

rm Deletes Files Immediately

The rm command does *not* move files into the trash. They are deleted *instantly* with no warning.[1] For a safer removal command, use rm -i which prompts before deletion:

> → rm -i myfile
> remove myfile? y

To make rm prompt before deletion all the time, put this alias into your *$HOME/.bash_profile* startup file:

> alias rm="/bin/rm -i"

then close and reopen your Terminal window.

Useful options

- -i   Interactive mode. Ask before deleting each file.

- -f   Force the deletion, ignoring any errors or warnings.

- -r   Recursively remove a directory and its contents. Use with caution, especially if combined with the -f option, as it can wipe out many files quickly.

---

ln

stdin   stdout   - file   **-- opt**   --help   --version

ln [*options*] *source target*

A *link* is a reference to another file, created by the ln command. Intuitively, links give the same file multiple names, allowing it to live in two (or more) locations at once.

There are two kinds of links. A *symbolic link* (also called a *symlink* or *soft link*) refers to another file by its path, much like a Macintosh "alias." To create a symbolic link, use the -s option:

> → ln -s myfile mysoftlink

---

1. A file removed by rm can theoretically be recovered by an undelete program. To remove a file more permanently, say, in a high-security environment, use the srm command instead. See man srm for details.

If you delete the original file, the now-dangling link will be invalid, pointing to a nonexistent file path. A *hard link*, on the other hand, is simply a *second name* for a physical file on disk (in tech talk, it points to the same *inode*).[2] If you delete the original file, the link still works as if it were the original file. Figure 2-1 illustrates the difference. To create a hard link, type:

→ `ln myfile myhardlink`

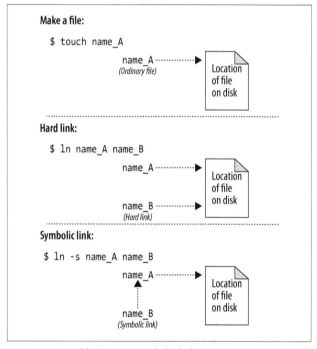

Figure 2-1. Hard link versus symbolic link

Symbolic links can point to files on other disk partitions, since they are just references to file paths; hard links cannot, since an inode

2. The *inode* of a file is its numeric ID on a disk partition.

on one disk has no meaning on another. Symbolic links can also point to directories, whereas hard links cannot.

Useful options

- -s Make a symbolic link. The default is a hard link.

- -i Interactive mode. Ask before overwriting destination files.

- -f Force the link. If a destination file exists, overwrite it unconditionally.

It's easy to find out where a symbolic link points with either of these commands:

```
→ readlink linkname
→ ls -l linkname
```

Links vs. Aliases

Symbolic links might seem similar to Macintosh aliases because they both point to files and folders. Aliases, however, work only in the Finder, while symbolic links work with all Macintosh applications, including the shell. If you create an alias to a folder, for example, you can open the alias in the Finder (which opens the folder), but you cannot cd into the alias from the shell. cd does follow symbolic links.

Using the ls -l command, you can examine how aliases and links appear in the filesystem. Here is a file *myfile* that has an alias *A* and a symbol link *L* that both point to it:

```
→ ls -l
-rw-r--r--@ 1 smith staff 0 Mar 18 21:43 A
lrwxr-xr-x  1 smith staff 6 Mar 18 21:42 L -> myfile
-rw-r--r--  1 smith staff 0 Mar 18 21:42 myfile
```

Alias *A* is displayed with an @ symbol next to its permissions, indicating that it has *extended attributes* that identify the target file, *myfile*. (We'll discuss extended attributes with the xattr command in "File Properties" on page 68.) The symbolic link *L* is displayed with an arrow (->) pointing to the target file.

Directory Operations

cd	Change your current directory.
pwd	Print the name of your current directory, i.e., "where you are now" in the filesystem.
basename	Print the final part of a file path.
dirname	Print the name of a directory that contains a file.
mkdir	Create (make) a directory.
rmdir	Delete (remove) an empty directory.
rm -r	Delete a nonempty directory and its contents.

We discussed the directory structure of OS X in "The Filesystem" on page 15. Now we'll cover commands that create, modify, delete, and manipulate directories within that structure.

---

cd   stdin   stdout   - file   -- opt   --help   --version

cd [*directory*]

The cd (change directory) command sets your current working directory. Using cd is like opening a particular shell's folder in the Finder, where you're ready to do work.

→ cd /usr/bin

With no directory supplied, cd defaults to your home directory:

→ cd

---

pwd   stdin   **stdout**   - file   -- opt   --help   --version

pwd

The pwd command prints the absolute path of your shell's current working directory:

→ pwd
/Users/smith/mydir

---

basename

basename *path* [*suffix*]

The basename command, given a file path, prints the final component in the path:

> → **basename /Users/smith/finances/money.txt**
> money.txt

If you provide an optional suffix, it gets stripped from the result:

> → **basename /Users/smith/finances/money.txt .txt**
> money

basename doesn't care if the file path exists: it just extracts the final filename.

---

dirname

dirname *path*

The dirname command, given a file path, prints the name of the directory that contains it:

> → **dirname /Users/smith/finances/money.txt**
> /Users/smith/finances

dirname does not change your current working directory, and it doesn't care if the path exists. It simply manipulates a file path string, just like basename does.

---

mkdir

mkdir [*options*] *directories*

mkdir creates one or more directories:

> → **mkdir directory1 directory2 directory3**

Useful options

-p   Given a directory path (not just a simple directory name), create any necessary parent directories automatically. The command:

> → **mkdir -p /one/two/three**

---

creates the directories */one* and */one/two* if they don't already exist, then */one/two/three*.

-m*mode*   Create the directory with the given permissions (explained more fully with the chmod and umask commands in "File Properties" on page 68):

> → mkdir -m 0755 mydir

By default, your shell's umask controls the permissions.

---

rmdir

rmdir [*options*] *directories*

The rmdir (remove directory) command deletes one or more empty directories you name:

> → rmdir /tmp/junk

Useful options

-p   If you supply a directory path (not just a simple directory name), delete not only the given directory, but the specified parent directories automatically, all of which must be empty. So the command:

> → rmdir -p one/two/three

will delete not only *one/two/three*, but also *one/two* and *one*.

To delete a nonempty directory and its contents, use (carefully) rm -r *directory*. Use rm -ri to delete interactively, or rm -rf to annihilate without any error messages or confirmation.

File Viewing

cat	View files in their entirety.
less	View text files one page at a time.
head	View the first lines of a text file.
tail	View the last lines of a text file.
nl	View text files with their lines numbered.
strings	Display text that's embedded in a binary file.

| od | View data in octal (or other formats). |
| xxd | View data in hexadecimal. |

On a Mac, you'll encounter various types of files to view: plain text, binary data, and more. Here we'll explain how to view them.

---

cat   stdin   stdout   - file   -- opt   --help   --version

`cat [options] [files]`

The simplest viewer is `cat`, which just prints its files to standard output, concatenating them (hence the name). Large files will likely scroll off screen, so consider using `less` if you plan to read the output. That being said, `cat` is particularly useful for sending a set of files into a shell pipeline like this one, which concatenates files in the current directory and counts the total number of lines:

    → `cat * | wc -l`

`cat` can also manipulate its output in small ways, optionally displaying nonprinting characters like carriage returns, prepending line numbers (though `nl` is more powerful for this purpose), and eliminating whitespace.

Useful options

- `-v`   Print any nonprinting characters (carriage returns, etc.) in a human-readable format.
- `-t`   Same as `-v`, and also print tabs as ^I.
- `-e`   Same as `-v`, and also print newlines as $.
- `-n`   Prepend line numbers to every line.
- `-b`   Prepend line numbers to nonblank lines.
- `-s`   Squeeze each sequence of blank lines into a single blank line.

less   stdin   stdout[3]   - file   -- opt   --help   --version

`less [options] [files]`

Use `less` to view text one "page" at a time (i.e., one window or screenful at a time). It's great for text files, or as the final command in a shell pipeline with lengthy output:

→ *command1* | *command2* | *command3* | *command4* | `less`

While running `less`, type h for a help message describing all its features. Here are some useful keystrokes for paging through files.

Keystroke	Meaning
q	Quit.
h, H	View a help page.
Space bar, f, ^V, ^F	Move forward one screenful.
Enter	Move forward one line.
b, ^B, ESC-v	Move backward one screenful.
/	Enter search mode. Follow it with a regular expression and press Enter, and `less` will look for the first line matching it.
?	Same as /, but it searches backward in the file.
n	Repeat your most recent search forward.
N	Repeat your most recent search backward.
v	Edit the current file with your default text editor (the value of environment variable VISUAL, or if not defined, EDITOR, or if not defined, vi).
<	Jump to beginning of file.
>	Jump to end of file.
:n	Jump to next file (if viewing multiple files).
:p	Jump to previous file (if viewing multiple files).

---

3. Although technically `less` can be plugged into the middle of a pipeline, or its output redirected to a file, there isn't much point to doing this.

less has a mind-boggling number of features; we're presenting only the most common. The manpage is recommended reading.

Useful options

- -c   Clear the screen before displaying the next page. This avoids scrolling and may be more comfortable on the eyes.

- -m   Print a more verbose prompt, displaying the percentage of the file displayed so far.

- -N   Display line numbers.

- -r   Display control characters literally; normally less converts them to a human-readable format.

- -s   Squeeze multiple, adjacent blank lines into a single blank line.

- -S   Truncate long lines to the width of the screen, instead of wrapping.

---

head

head [options] [files]

The head command prints the first 10 lines of a file: great for previewing the contents of a file:

→ **head myfile**

or of many files, with a convenient header in front of each:

→ **head * | less**   *Preview all files in the current directory*

or the first few lines of output from a pipeline. Here we use the grep command (see "File Text Manipulation" on page 81), which locates matching lines in a file, to print all lines containing a capital E. by piping the output to head, we display only the first 10 matches:

→ **grep 'E' very-big-file | head**

Useful options

- -*N*   Print the first *N* lines instead of 10.

- -n *N*   Print the first *N* lines instead of 10.

- -c *N*   Print the first *N* bytes of the file.

tail

stdin   stdout   - file   -- opt   --help   --version

`tail [options] [files]`

The `tail` command prints the last 10 lines of a file, and does other tricks as well:

>   → **tail myfile**

The ultra-useful `-f` option causes `tail` to watch a file actively while another program is writing to it, displaying new lines as they are written to the file. This is invaluable for watching log files as they grow:

>   → **tail -f /var/log/messages**

Useful options

`-N`	Print the last N lines of the file instead of the last 10.
`-n N`	Print the last N lines of the file instead of the last 10.
`-n +N`	Print all lines except the first N.
`-c N`	Print the last N bytes of the file.
`-f`	Keep the file open, and whenever lines are appended to the file, print them. This is extremely useful. Add the `--retry` option if the file doesn't exist yet, but you want to wait for it to exist.
`-q`	Quiet mode: when processing more than one file, don't print a banner above each file. Normally `tail` prints a banner containing the filename.

nl

stdin   stdout   - file   -- opt   --help   --version

`nl [options] [files]`

nl copies its files to standard output, prepending line numbers:

>   → **nl myfile**
>   ```
>       1  Once upon a time, there was
>       2  a little operating system named
>       3  OS X, which everybody loved.
>   ```

It's more flexible than `cat` with its `-n` and `-b` options, providing an almost bizarre amount of control over the numbering. nl can be used in two ways: on ordinary text files, and on specially marked-up text files with predefined headers and footers.

Useful options

-b [a|t|n|pR]	Prepend numbers to all lines (a), nonblank lines (t), no lines (n), or only lines that contain regular expression R. (Default = a)
-v N	Begin numbering with integer N. (Default = 1)
-i N	Increment the number by N for each line, so for example, you could use odd numbers only (-i2) or even numbers only (-v2 -i2). (Default = 1)
-n [ln|rn|rz]	Format numbers as left-justified (ln), right-justified (rn), or right-justified with leading zeroes (rz). (Default = ln)
-w N	Force the width of the number to be N columns. (Default = 6)
-s S	Insert string S between the line number and the text. (Default = Tab)

Additionally, nl has the wacky ability to divide text files into virtual pages, each with a header, body, and footer with different numbering schemes. For this to work, however, you must insert nl-specific delimiter strings into the file, such as \:\:\: (start of header), \: \: (start of body), and \: (start of footer). Each must appear on a line by itself. Then you can use additional options (see the manpage) to affect line numbering in the headers and footers of your decorated file.

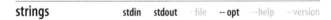

strings   stdin stdout -file --opt --help --version

```
strings [options] [files]
```

Binary files, such as executable programs and object files, usually contain some readable text. The strings program extracts that text and displays it on standard output. You can discover version information, authors' names, and other useful tidbits with strings:

```
→ strings /usr/bin/who
$NetBSD: who.c,v 1.23 2008/07/24 15:35:41 christos Exp $
Copyright (c) 1989, 1993 The Regents of the University of
 California...
```

Combine strings and grep (a command that locates matching lines in a file; see "File Text Manipulation" on page 81) to make your exploring more efficient. Here we look for email addresses in the binary file for the emacs editor by searching for @ signs:

```
→ strings /usr/bin/emacs | grep '@'
bug-gnu-emacs@gnu.org
```

Useful options

-n *length*   Display only strings with length greater than *length* (the default = 4).

---

od   **stdin**   **stdout**   - file   **-- opt**   --help   --version

od [*options*] [*files*]

When you want to view a binary file, consider od (Octal Dump) for the job. It copies one or more files to standard output, displaying their data in ASCII, octal (base 8), decimal, hexadecimal (base 16), or floating point, in various sizes (byte, short, long). For example, this command:

```
→ od /usr/bin/who
0000000    177312  137272  000000  001000  ...
0000020    000000  000020  000000  060114  ...
0000040    000000  001400  000000  000140  ...
...
```

displays the bytes in binary file */usr/bin/who* in octal. The column on the left contains the file offset of each row, again in octal.

If your binary file also contains text, consider the -tc option, which displays character data:

```
→ od -tc /usr/bin/who | head -3
0000000  312 376 272 276  \0  \0  \0 002 001  \0 ...
0000020   \0  \0 020  \0  \0  \0   L   `  \0  \0 ...
0000040   \0  \0  \0 003  \0  \0   `  \0  \0  \0 ...
```

Useful options

-N *B*   Display only the first *B* bytes of each file.

-j *B*   Begin the output at byte *B* +1 of each file. You can append the letter b to skip blocks instead of bytes, k for kilobytes, or m for megabytes.

-A (d|o|x|n)	Display file offsets in the leftmost column, in decimal (d), octal (o), hexadecimal (h), or not at all (n). (Default = o)
-t (a|c)	Display output in a character format, with non-alphanumeric characters printed as escape sequences (c) or by name (a).
-t (d|o|u|x) [SIZE]	Display output in an integer format, including octal (o), signed decimal (d), unsigned decimal (u), hexadecimal (x). (For binary output, use xxd instead.) SIZE represents the number of bytes per integer; it can be a positive integer or any of the values C, S, I, or L, which stand for the size of a char, short, int, or long datatype, respectively.
-t f[SIZE]	Display output in floating point. SIZE represents the number of bytes per integer; it can be a positive integer or any of the values F, D, or L, which stand for the size of a float, double, or long double datatype, respectively.
	If -t is omitted, the default is -to2.

xxd

stdin   stdout   - file   -- opt   --help   --version

xxd [options] [files]

Similar to od, xxd produces a hexadecimal or binary dump of a file in several different formats. It can also do the reverse, converting from its hex dump format back into the original data. For example, here's a hex dump of binary file /usr/bin/who:

```
→ xxd /usr/bin/who
0000000: cafe babe 0000 0002 0100 ... 0003  ...............
0000010: 0000 1000 0000 4c60 0000 ... 0007  ......L`........
0000020: 0000 0003 0000 6000 0000 ... 000c  ......`...K.....
...
```

The left column indicates the file offset of the row, the next eight columns contain the data, and the final column displays the printable characters in the row, if any.

By default, xxd outputs three columns: file offsets, the data in hex, and the data as text (printable characters only).

Useful options

-l N	Display only the first N bytes. (Default displays the entire file.)

-s *N*	Skip the first *N* bytes of the file.
-s -*N*	Begin *N* bytes from the end of the file. (There is also a +*N* syntax for more advanced skipping through standard input; see the manpage.)
-c *N*	Display *N* bytes per row. (Default = 16)
-g *N*	Group each row of bytes into sequences of *N* bytes, separated by whitespace, like od -s. (Default = 2)
-b	Display the output in binary instead of hexadecimal.
-u	Display the output in uppercase hexadecimal instead of lowercase.
-p	Display the output as a plain hex dump, 60 contiguous bytes per line.
-r	The reverse operation: convert from an xxd hex dump back into the original file format. Works with the default hex dump format and, if you add the -p option, the plain hex dump format. If you're bored, try either of these commands to convert and unconvert a file in a pipeline, reproducing the original file on standard output: → xxd myfile | xxd -r → xxd -p myfile | xxd -r -p
-i	Display the output as a C programming language data structure. When reading from a file, it produces an array of unsigned chars containing the data, and an unsigned int containing the array length. When reading from standard input, it produces only a comma-separated list of hex bytes.

File Creation and Editing

Command	Meaning
emacs	Text editor from Free Software Foundation.
vim	Text editor, extension of Unix vi.
look	Print dictionary words on standard output.

To make best use of the Terminal, you must become proficient with a text editor available from the command line. For editing the plain text files you'll need for shell operations, word processors such as Microsoft Word and Apple's TextEdit are not appropriate because they insert invisible text-formatting characters into the files.[4] Plus they are graphical applications that run only on the Mac's monitor, so they won't work for remote logins (for more information, see "Running a Shell Remotely" on page 183). The two major editors are Emacs from the Free Software Foundation, and vim, a successor to the Unix editor vi.[5] Teaching these editors fully is beyond the scope of this book, but both have online tutorials, and we list common operations in Table 2-1. To edit a file, run either:

```
➜ emacs myfile
➜ vim myfile
```

If *myfile* doesn't exist, it is created automatically the first time you save.

Creating a File Quickly

You can quickly create an empty file (for later editing) using the **touch** command, providing a filename that does not exist (see "File Properties" on page 68):

---

4. Technically, you can use TextEdit if you save its file in the format "Plain Text." If you don't, other shell commands will not operate properly on these files.

5. Another available editor is pico, which is simpler than Emacs and vim but more limited: see **man pico** for details.

```
→ touch newfile
```

Another quick technique uses the echo command with the -n option, redirecting its output to a new file. This option prevents a newline character from being echoed, making the file truly empty:

```
→ echo -n > newfile2
```

You can also write data into a new file by redirecting the output of a program (see "Input/output redirection" on page 32):

```
→ echo anything at all > newfile
```

If you accidentally provide the name of an existing file, **touch** will preserve it but redirecting echo will erase its contents. So be careful!

Your Default Editor

Various shell commands will run an editor when necessary, and by default the editor is vim. For example, a text-based email program may invoke an editor to compose a new message, and **less** invokes an editor if you type "v". But what if you don't want vim to be your default editor? Set the environment variables VISUAL and EDITOR to your choice, for example:

```
→ EDITOR=emacs
→ VISUAL=emacs
→ export EDITOR VISUAL            Optional
```

Both variables are necessary because different programs check one variable or the other. Set EDITOR and VISUAL in your *$HOME/.bash_profile* startup file, then close and reopen your Terminal window, if you want your choices made permanent.

Regardless of how you set these variables, all system administrators should know at least basic vim and Emacs commands in case a system tool suddenly runs an editor on a critical file.

Emacs   stdin   stdout   - file   -- opt   **--help**   **--version**

emacs [*options*] [*files*]

Emacs is an extremely powerful editing environment with more commands than you could possibly imagine, plus a complete programming language to define your own editing features. To run Emacs in a Terminal window, run:

→ `emacs`

Now to invoke the built-in Emacs tutorial, type ^h t.

Most Emacs keystroke commands involve the control key (like ^F) or the *meta* key, which is usually the Escape key or the Option key. Emacs's own documentation notates the meta key as M- (as in M-F to mean "hold the meta key and type F"), so we will too. For basic keystrokes, see Table 2-1.

---

vim   stdin   stdout   **- file**   **-- opt**   --help   --version

`vim [options] [files]`

vim is an enhanced version of the old standard Unix editor vi. To invoke the editor in a Terminal window, run:

→ `vim`

To take the vim tutorial, run:

→ `vimtutor`

vim is a mode-based editor. It operates in two modes, *insert* and *normal*. Insert mode is for entering text in the usual manner, while normal mode is for running commands like "delete a line" or copy/paste. For basic keystrokes in normal mode, see Table 2-1.

Table 2-1. Basic keystrokes in Emacs and vim

Task	Emacs	vim
Type some text	Just type	Type i, then any text, and finally Esc
Save and quit	^x^s then ^x^c	:wq
Quit without saving	^x^c	:q!
	Respond "no" when asked to save buffers	
Save	^x^s	:w
Save As	^x^w	:w *filename*
Undo	^/ or ^x u	u
Suspend editor (not in X)	^z	^z
Switch to edit mode	(*N/A*)	Esc
Switch to command mode	M-x	:
Abort command in progress	^g	Esc
Move forward	^f or right arrow	l or right arrow
Move backward	^b or left arrow	h or left arrow
Move up	^p or up arrow	k or up arrow
Move down	^n or down arrow	j or down arrow
Move to next word	M-f	w
Move to previous word	M-b	b
Move to beginning of line	^a	0
Move to end of line	^e	$
Move down one screen	^v	^f
Move up one screen	M-v	^b
Move to beginning of buffer	M-<	gg
Move to end of buffer	M->	G
Delete next character	^d	x
Delete previous character	Backspace	X

Task	Emacs	vim
Delete next word	M-d	de
Delete previous word	M-Backspace	db
Delete current line	^a^k	dd
Delete to end of line	^k	d$
Define region (type this keystroke to mark the beginning of the region, then move the cursor to the end of the desired region)	^ Space bar	v
Cut region	^w	d
Copy region	M-w	y
Paste region	^y	p
Get help	^h	:help
View the manual	^h i	:help

---

look

stdin · **stdout** · - file · **-- opt** · --help · --version

```
look [options] prefix [dictionary_file]
```

While writing in your text editor, consider the look command in a second Terminal window for quickly looking up the spelling of words. It prints words that begin with a given string (case-insensitively). The words come from a dictionary file, */usr/share/dict/ words*. For instance, the command:

→ **look bigg**

prints all words in the dictionary file that begin with those letters:

```
bigg
biggah
biggen
bigger
biggest
...
```

If you supply your own dictionary file—any text file with alphabetically sorted lines—look will print all dictionary lines that begin with the given prefix.

Useful options

-f   Ignore case.

-t *X*   Match the prefix only up to and including the termination character *X*. For instance, `look -ti big` prints all words beginning with "bi."

File Properties

stat   Display attributes of files and directories.

wc   Count bytes, words, lines in a file.

du   Measure disk usage of files and directories.

file   Identify (guess) the type of a file.

touch   Change timestamps of files and directories.

chown   Change owner of files and directories.

chgrp   Change group ownership of files and directories.

chmod   Change protection mode of files and directories.

umask   Set a default mode for new files and directories.

xattr   Work with extended attributes of files and directories.

When examining a file, keep in mind that the contents are just part of the story. Every file and directory also has attributes that describe its owner, size, access permissions, and other information. The `ls -l` command (see "Basic File Operations" on page 45) displays some of these attributes, but other commands provide additional information.

---

stat   stdin   **stdout**   - file   **-- opt**   --help   --version

stat [*options*] *files*

The `stat` command displays important attributes of files. By default, file information is printed in one long line:

```
→ stat myfile
234881026 3004666 -rw-r--r-- 1 lisa staff 0 1264 ...
```

---

but you can display it in a more friendly manner with the -x option:

```
→ stat -x myfile
  File: "myfile"
  Size: 1264          FileType: Regular File
  Mode: (0644/-rw-r--r--) Uid: (501/lisa) Gid: (20/staff)
Device: 14,2   Inode: 3004666    Links: 1
Access: Sun Mar 11 20:31:53 2012
Modify: Wed Mar  7 22:05:56 2012
Change: Wed Mar  7 22:05:56 2012
```

This includes the filename, size in bytes (1,264), file type (Regular File), permissions in octal (0644), permissions in the format of "ls -l" (-rw-r--r--), owner's user ID (501), owner's name (lisa), owner's group ID (20), owner's group name (staff), device information (14,2), inode number (3004666), number of hard links (1), and timestamps of the file's most recent access, modification, and status change.

Useful options

-L	Follow symbolic links and report on the file they point to.
-x	Display the results in a friendly, readable format.
-f *format*	Display the results in a highly configurable format; see the manpage for details.

WC   stdin   stdout   -file   --opt   --help   --version

wc [*options*] [*files*]

The wc (word count) program prints a count of bytes, words, and lines in a plain text file.[6]

```
→ wc myfile
    24      62     428 myfile
```

This file has 24 lines, 62 whitespace-delimited words, and 428 bytes.

---

6. You can run wc on a nontext file, but the concepts of "lines" and "words" will not be well defined.

Useful options

- `-l`   Print the line count only.

- `-w`   Print the word count only.

- `-c`   Print the byte count only.

---

du

`du [options] [files| directories]`

The du (disk usage) command measures the disk space occupied by files or directories. By default, it measures the current directory and all its subdirectories, printing totals in blocks for each, with a grand total at the bottom:

```
→ du
6213880      ./Desktop
6440952      ./Documents
14237024     ./Downloads
430300       ./Library
11408        ./Library/Application Support
0            ./Library/Assistants
...
77797648     .
```

It can also measure the size of files:

```
→ du myfile myfile2
4    myfile
16   myfile2
```

Useful options

- `-k`   Measure usage in kilobytes.

- `-m`   Measure usage in megabytes.

- `-g`   Measure usage in gigabytes.

- `-h`   Print in human-readable units. For example, if two directories are of size 1 gigabyte or 25 kilobytes, respectively, du -h prints 1G and 25K.

- `-c`   Print a total in the last line. This is the default behavior when measuring a directory, but for measuring individual files, provide -c if you want a total.

- `-L`   Follow symbolic links and measure the files they point to.

-s   Print only the total size.

---

file

file [options] files

The file command reports the type of a file:

```
→ file /etc/hosts /usr/bin/who letter.doc
/etc/hosts:    ASCII English text
/usr/bin/who:  Mach-O universal binary …
letter.doc:    CDF V2 Document, Little Endian, Os: MacOS …
```

The reported file types are not always accurate; the file program has its roots in older operating systems that don't track true file types the way the Macintosh does. The output is an educated guess based on file content and other factors.

Useful options

-b	Omit filenames (left column of output).
-I	Print MIME types for the file, such as "text/plain" or "audio/mpeg," instead of the usual output.
-f name_file	Read filenames, one per line, from the given name_file, and report their types. Afterward, process filenames on the command line as usual.
-L	Follow symbolic links, reporting the type of the destination file instead of the link.
-z	If a file is compressed (see "File Compression and Packaging" on page 102), examine the uncompressed contents to decide the file type, instead of reporting "compressed data."

---

touch

touch [options] files

The touch command changes two timestamps associated with a file: its modification time (when the file's data was last changed) and its access time (when the file was last read). To set both timestamps to right now, run:

→ **touch** `myfile`

You can set these timestamps to arbitrary values, e.g., to set its timestamp to March 15, 2012, at noon:

→ **touch -t** `201203151200` **myfile**

If a given file doesn't exist, touch creates it—a handy way to create empty files.

Useful options

-a	Change the access time only.
-m	Change the modification time only.
-c	If the file doesn't exist, don't create it (normally, touch creates it).
-t *timestamp*	Set the file's *timestamp*, using the format *[[CC]YY]MMDDhhmm [.ss]*, where *CC* is the two-digit century, *YY* is the two-digit year, *MM* is the two-digit month, *DD* is the two-digit day, *hh* is the two-digit hour, *mm* is the two-digit minute, and *ss* is the two-digit second. For example, -t 20030812150047 represents August 12, 2003, at 15:00:47.

---

chown

stdin   stdout   - file   -- opt   --help   --version

chown [*options*] *user_spec files*

The chown (change owner) command sets the ownership of files and directories. To make user smith the owner of several files and a directory, run:

→ **sudo chown smith myfile myfile2 mydir**

The *user_spec* parameter may be any of these possibilities:

- A username (or numeric user ID), to set the owner: chown smith myfile
- A username (or numeric user ID), optionally followed by a colon and a group name (or numeric group ID), to set the owner and group: chown smith:users myfile
- A username (or numeric user ID) followed by a colon, to set the owner *and* to set the group to the invoking user's login group: chown smith: myfile

---

- A group name (or numeric group ID) preceded by a colon, to set the group only: `chown :users myfile`. This is equivalent to `chgrp users myfile`; see "Group Management" on page 147.

Useful options

-h If the file is a symbolic link, change the link itself, not the file it points to.

-R Recursively change the ownership within a directory hierarchy.

---

chgrp

stdin   stdout   - file   -- opt   --help   --version

`chgrp [options] group_spec files`

The chgrp (change group) command sets the group ownership of files and directories:

→ `chgrp staff myfile myfile2 mydir`

The *group_spec* parameter may be a group name or numeric group ID. See "Group Management" on page 147 for more information on groups.

Useful options

-h If the file is a symbolic link, change the link itself, not the file it points to.

-R Recursively change the ownership within a directory hierarchy.

---

chmod

stdin   stdout   - file   -- opt   --help   --version

`chmod [options] permissions files`

The chmod (change mode) command protects files and directories from unauthorized access in the filesystem by setting access permissions. We described these permissions—read (r), write (w), and execute (x)—in "File Protections" on page 24. These permissions are described as a string of nine characters (rwxrwxrwx) consisting of three triplets: the first for the user owning the file, the second for group ownership, and the third for other users.

For example, here we have a file *myfile* that is readable and writable by its owner, readable by its group, and readable by others:

```
→ ls -l myfile
-rw-r--r--  1 smith  staff  4 Apr 26 22:22 myfile
```

Using chmod, we can take away the read permissions for the group (g) and the other users (o):

```
→ chmod g-r,o-r myfile
→ ls -l myfile
-rw-------  1 smith  staff  4 Apr 26 22:23 myfile
```

Now we make the file read-only for all users (a):

```
→ chmod a=r myfile
→ ls -l myfile
-r--r--r--  1 smith  staff  4 Apr 26 22:24 myfile
```

chmod understands permissions in two formats, one numeric, and one symbolic, as depicted in Figure 2-2.

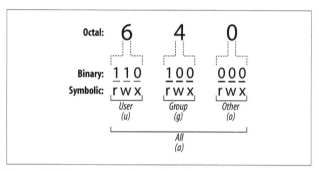

Figure 2-2. File permission bits explained

Numeric format

Each triplet rwx can be represented by a number. Imagine that the digit 1 means a permission is present and zero means absent. So read-only permission would be 100 (meaning r--), read and write together would be 110 (meaning rw-), and execute alone would be 001 (meaning --x). In all, there are eight possibilities from 000 (---) to 111 (rwx).

These eight binary values can be written as the digits 0 to 7, as in Figure 2-2.[7] To cover all three triplets, you'll need three digits. For example, the value 640 is the same as 110100000 in binary, which represents the permissions rw-r-----. Using these ideas, you can set a file's *absolute* permissions in bits:

```
→ chmod 640 myfile
→ ls -l myfile
-rw-r-----  1 smith  staff  4 Apr 26 22:24 myfile
```

This three-digit value is sometimes called the *mode* of a file (e.g., "I created that file with mode 640"). Some common modes for files are:

400	Readable only by the owner
444	Read-only by everyone
600	Read/write only by the owner
644	Readable by everyone, writable only by the owner

Some common modes for directories are:

700	Only the owner can read, write, and enter the directory.
750	Owner and group may read and enter the directory, but only the owner can write.
755	Everyone may read and enter the directory, but only the owner can write.

Symbolic format

You can also set a file's permissions using a string of letters (like r for read permission) and symbols (like = to set permissions). Recall our previous example that made a file read-only by all users:

```
→ chmod a=r myfile
```

The permissions string has three parts:

Whose permission?

u for user, g for group, o for other users not in the group, a for all users. The default is a.

---

7. Technically these digits are in base 8, a.k.a. octal numbers.

Add, remove, or set?
> + to add permissions; - to remove permissions; or = to set absolute permissions, overwriting existing ones.

Which permissions?
> r for read, w for write/modify, x and for execute (for directories, this is permission to cd into the directory).

> You can also use the shorthand u to duplicate the owner permissions, g to duplicate the group permissions, or o to duplicate the (world) permissions.

> Several other characters are described in the upcoming section "Advanced permissions" on page 76.

For example, to add read and write permission for the user and the group, run:

→ chmod ug+rw myfile

To remove execute permission for all users, run either of these commands, which are equivalent:

→ chmod a-x myfile
→ chmod -x myfile

To create entirely new permissions (deleting the old ones) and make a file readable only by its owner, run:

→ chmod u=r myfile

You can combine permission strings by separating them with commas, such as ug+rw,a-x.

Advanced permissions

chmod has other permissions that it can manipulate. See the manpage for more information on these less common permissions:

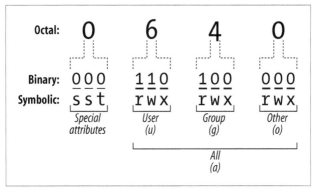

Figure 2-3. Advanced file permission bits

- Setuid and setgid (**s**) apply to executable files (programs and scripts). Suppose we have an executable file *myprogram* owned by user "smith" and the group "friends." If file *myprogram* has setuid (set user ID) enabled, then anyone who runs *myprogram* will "become" user smith, with all her rights and privileges, for the duration of the program. Examples:

```
→ chmod u+s myprogram
→ chmod 4755 myprogram
→ ls -l myprogram
-rwsr-xr-x 1 smith staff 8570 Apr 30 22:58 myprogram
```

  Likewise, if *myprogram* has setgid (set group ID) enabled, anyone who executes *myprogram* becomes a member of the friends group for the duration of the program:

```
→ chmod g+s myprogram
→ chmod 2755 myprogram
→ ls -l myprogram
-rwxr-sr-x 1 smith staff 8570 Apr 30 22:58 myprogram
```

  As you might imagine, setuid and setgid can impact system security, so don't use them unless you *really* know what you're doing. One misplaced chmod +s can leave your whole system vulnerable to attack.

- The sticky bit (**t**), most commonly used for */tmp* directories, controls removal of files in that directory. Normally, if you have write permission in a directory, you can delete or move files within it, even if you don't have this access to the files themselves. Inside a directory with the sticky bit set, you also need write permission on a file in order to delete or move it:

```
→ chmod +t mydirectory
→ chmod 1755 mydirectory
→ ls -ld mydirectory
drwxr-xr-t 2 smith staff 68 Apr 30 22:59 mydirectory
```

• Conditional execute permission (X, not shown in Figure 2-3) means the same as x, except that it succeeds only if the file is already executable, or if the file is a directory. Otherwise, it has no effect. Example:

```
→ chmod +X myfile
```

Useful options

-h   If the file is a symbolic link, change the link itself, not the file it points to.

-R   Recursively change the permissions within a directory hierarchy.

---

umask

stdin   **stdout**   - file   -- opt   --help   --version

```
umask [options] [mask]
```

The umask command sets or displays your default permission mode for creating files and directories: whether they are readable, writable, and/or executable by yourself, your group, and the world:

```
→ umask                  Display as octal number
0002
→ umask -S               Display as characters
u=rwx,g=rwx,o=rx
```

Your umask specifies permissions to be *removed* by default from files and directories you create. With a umask value of zero, files get created with mode 666 (rw-rw-rw) and directories with mode 777 (rwxrwxrwx).[8] Any other umask value gets *subtracted* from these default modes. For example, if you set your umask to 002:

```
→ umask 002
```

---

8. As with the chmod command, these modes are in base 8, a.k.a. octal numbers.

---

your default mode for files will be 666 minus 002, or 664, which is
rw-rw-r--. For directories, it will be 777 minus 002, or 775, which
is rwx-r-xr-x.

Here are some common values for your umask. Use mask 0022 to
give yourself full privileges, and all others read/execute privileges
only:

```
→ umask 0022
→ touch newfile1 && mkdir dir1
→ ls -ld newfile1 dir1
drwxr-xr-x    2 smith staff       4096 Nov 11 12:25 dir1
-rw-r--r--    1 smith staff          0 Nov 11 12:25 newfile1
```

Use mask 0002 to give yourself and your default group full privileges, and read/execute to others:

```
→ umask 0002
→ touch newfile2 && mkdir dir2
→ ls -ld newfile2 dir2
drwxrwxr-x    2 smith staff       4096 Nov 11 12:26 dir2
-rw-rw-r--    1 smith staff          0 Nov 11 12:26 newfile2
```

Use mask 0077 to give yourself full privileges with nothing for anyone else:

```
→ umask 0077
→ touch newfile3 && mkdir dir3
→ ls -ld newfile3 dir3
drwx------    2 smith staff       4096 Nov 11 12:27 dir3
-rw-------    1 smith staff          0 Nov 11 12:27 newfile3
```

Your umask affects only your current shell. To change the value for
all future shells, add a umask line to your $HOME/.bash_profile con-
figuration file, then close and reopen your Terminal window.

```
xattr [-[cdpw]] [options] attributes [files]
```

Files in OS X can have not only "normal" attributes, such as read, write, and execute permission, but also *extended attributes*, which can be any file metadata you dream up. Extended attributes are created and manipulated with the xattr command. For example, let's define an attribute called com.example.color, assign it the value blue, and apply it to the file *myfile*:[9]

```
→ touch myfile                          Create an empty file
→ xattr -w com.example.color blue myfile
```

Now list the file and look for the @ symbol in the output, indicating that extended attributes are present:

```
→ ls -l@ myfile
-rw-r--r--@ 1 smith  staff  0 Mar 26 22:19 myfile
```

and display its extended attribute values with xattr:

```
→ xattr -l myfile
com.example.color: blue
```

or just one attribute alone, by name:

```
→ xattr -p com.example.color myfile
blue
```

You can delete one attribute with -d:

```
→ xattr -d com.example.color myfile
```

or all of them with -c:

```
→ xattr -c myfile
```

While you can amuse yourself all day by creating and viewing attributes, their practical use is for Macintosh applications to store important data about files. For instance, the Finder maintains an extended attribute named com.apple.FinderInfo, displayed here in hexadecimal:

```
→ xattr -l letter.docx
00000000  57 58 42 4E 4D 53 57 44 00 ...
```

9. Extended attributes follow Java-style naming conventions, sort of like Internet hostnames in reverse order.

Useful options

- `-l` Display both the name and value of attributes, not just one or the other.

- `-r` Recursively operate on all files in a directory.

- `-s` Do not follow symbolic links: operate on the links themselves, not the destination files they point to.

Two other programs for managing extended attributes are GetFileInfo for listing attributes:

```
→ GetFileInfo myfile
file: "/Users/smith/Documents/myfile"
type: "\0\0\0\0"
creator: "\0\0\0\0"
attributes: avbstclinmedz
created: 04/14/2012 07:53:29
modified: 04/14/2012 07:53:29
```

and SetFile for changing them; for example, you can lock a file, preventing deletion, with:

```
→ SetFile -aL myfile
```

GetFileInfo and SetFile are not provided with OS X but can be added by installing Xcode, as described in "Installing Command Line Tools for Xcode" on page 188.

File Text Manipulation

grep   Find lines in a file that match a regular expression.

cut   Extract columns from a file.

paste Append columns.

tr   Translate characters into other characters.

sort   Sort lines of text by various criteria.

uniq   Locate identical lines in a file.

tee   Copy a file *and* print it on standard output, simultaneously.

Commands are terrific for text manipulation: manipulating a text file (or standard input) into a desired form by applying transformations, often in a pipeline. Any program that reads standard input and writes standard output falls into this category, but here we'll present some of the most important tools.

---

grep   stdin   stdout   - file   -- opt   --help   --version

```
grep [options] pattern [files]
```

The grep command is one of the most consistently useful and powerful in the Terminal arsenal. Its premise is simple: given one or more files, print all lines in those files that match a particular regular expression pattern. For example, if a file *myfile* contains these lines:

```
The quick brown fox jumped over the lazy dogs!
My very eager mother just served us nine pancakes.
Film at eleven.
```

and we search for all lines containing "pancake," we get:

```
→ grep pancake myfile
My very eager mother just served us nine pancakes.
```

grep also understands regular expressions: special strings for matching text in a file. Here we match lines ending in an exclamation point:

```
→ grep '\!$' myfile
The quick brown fox jumped over the lazy dogs!
```

grep can use two different types of regular expressions, which it calls *basic* and *extended*. They are equally powerful, just different, and you may prefer one over the other based on your experience with other grep implementations. The basic syntax is in Table 2-2.

Useful options

-v	Print only lines that *do not* match the regular expression.
-l	Print only the *names* of files that contain matching lines, not the lines themselves.
-L	Print only the names of files that *do not* contain matching lines.
-c	Print only a count of matching lines.
-n	In front of each line of matching output, print its original line number.

-b	In front of each line of matching output, print the byte offset of the line in the input file.
-i	Case-insensitive match.
-w	Match only complete words (i.e., words that match the entire regular expression).
-x	Match only complete lines (i.e., lines that match the entire regular expression). Overrides -w.
-A N	After each matching line, print the next N lines from its file.
-B N	Before each matching line, print the previous N lines from its file.
-C N	Same as -A N -B N: print N lines (from the original file) above *and* below each matching line.
--color=always	Highlight the matched text in color, for better readability.
-r	Recursively search all files in a directory and its subdirectories.
-E	Use extended regular expressions. See egrep.
-F	Use lists of fixed strings instead of regular expressions. See fgrep.

---

egrep   stdin   stdout   - file   -- opt   --help   --version

egrep [*options*] *pattern* [*files*]

The egrep command is just like grep, but uses a different ("extended") language for regular expressions. It's the same as grep -E.

Table 2-2. Regular expressions for grep and egrep

Regular expression

Plain	Extended	Meaning
.		Any single character.
[...]		Match any single character in this list.
[^...]		Match any single character NOT in this list.
(...)		Grouping.
|	|	Or.
^		Beginning of a line.

Regular expression

Plain	Extended	Meaning
`$`		End of a line.
`\<`		Beginning of a word.
`\>`		End of a word.
`[:alnum:]`		Any alphanumeric character.
`[:alpha:]`		Any alphabetic character.
`[:cntrl:]`		Any control character.
`[:digit:]`		Any digit.
`[:graph:]`		Any graphic character.
`[:lower:]`		Any lowercase letter.
`[:print:]`		Any printable character.
`[:punct:]`		Any punctuation mark.
`[:space:]`		Any whitespace character.
`[:upper:]`		Any uppercase letter.
`[:xdigit:]`		Any hexadecimal digit.
`*`		Zero or more repetitions of a regular expression.
`\+`	`+`	One or more repetitions of a regular expression.
`\?`	`?`	Zero or one occurrence of a regular expression.
`\{`*n*`\}`	`{`*n*`}`	Exactly *n* repetitions of a regular expression.
`\{`*n*`,\}`	`{`*n*`,}`	*n* or more repetitions of a regular expression.
`\{`*n*`,`*m*`\}`	`{`*n*`,`*m*`}`	Between *n* and *m* (inclusive) repetitions of a regular expression, *n* < *m*.
`\`*c*		The character *c* literally, even if *c* is a special regular expression character. For example, use `\*` to match an asterisk or `\\` to match a backslash. Alternatively, put the literal character inside square brackets, like `[*]` or `[\]`.

grep and End-of-Line Characters

When you match the end of a line ($) with grep, text files created on Linux or Microsoft Windows systems may produce odd results on a Mac. The reason is that each operating system has a different standard for ending a line. On Windows, each line in a text file ends with a two-character sequence: a carriage return (ASCII 13) followed by a newline character (ASCII 10). On Linux, each line ends with only a newline. And in OS X, a text file might end its lines with newlines or carriage returns alone. If grep isn't matching the ends of lines properly, check the end-of-line characters with cat -v, which displays carriage returns as ^M:

```
→ cat -v dosfile
Uh-oh! This file seems to end its lines with^M
carriage returns before the newlines.^M
```

To remove the carriage returns, use the tr -d command:

```
→ tr -d '\r' < dosfile > newfile
→ cat -v newfile
Uh-oh! This file seems to end its lines with
carriage returns before the newlines.
```

---

fgrep   stdin   stdout   - file   -- opt   --help   --version

fgrep [options] [fixed_strings] [files]

The fgrep command is just like grep, but instead of accepting a regular expression, it accepts a list of fixed strings, separated by newlines. It's the same as grep -F. For example, if you have a dictionary file full of strings, one per line:

```
→ cat my_dictionary_file
aardvark
aback
abandon
...
```

you can conveniently search for those strings in a set of input files:

```
→ fgrep -f my_dictionary_file inputfile1 inputfile2
```

Normally, you'll use the lowercase -f option to make fgrep read the fixed strings from a file. You can also read the fixed strings on the command line using quoting, but it's a bit trickier. To search for the strings one, two, and three in a file, you'd type:

→ **fgrep** 'one   *Note we are typing newline characters*
two
three' myfile

fgrep is convenient when searching for non-alphanumeric characters like * and { because they are taken literally, not as regular expression characters.

---

cut   stdin   stdout   - file   -- opt   --help   --version

cut -(b|c|f)*range* [*options*] [*files*]

The cut command extracts columns of text from files. A "column" is defined by character offsets (e.g., the nineteenth character of each line):

→ **cut -c19 myfile**

or by byte offsets (which are often the same as characters, unless you have multibyte characters in your language):

→ **cut -b19 myfile**

or by delimited fields (e.g., the fifth field in each line of a comma-delimited file):

→ **cut -f5 -d, myfile**

You aren't limited to printing a single column: you can provide a range (3-16), a comma-separated sequence (3,4,5,6,8,16), or both (3,4,8-16). For ranges, if you omit the first number (-16), a 1 is assumed (1-16); if you omit the last number (5-), the end of line is used.

Useful options

-d *C*   Use character *C* as the *input* delimiter character between fields for the - f option. By default it's a Tab character.

-s   Suppress (don't print) lines that don't contain the delimiter character.

---

paste stdin   stdout   - file   -- opt   --help   --version

```
paste [options] [files]
```

The paste command is the opposite of cut: it treats several files as
vertical columns and combines them on standard output, effectively
pasting them side by side:

```
→ cat letters
A
B
C
→ cat numbers
1
2
3
4
5
→ paste numbers letters
1   A
2   B
3   C
4
5
→ paste letters numbers
A   1
B   2
C   3
    4
    5
```

Useful options

-d *delimiters*	Use the given *delimiters* characters between columns; the default is a Tab character. Provide a single character (-d:) to be used always, or a list of characters (-dxyz) to be applied in sequence on each line (the first delimiter is x, then y, then z, then x, then y, . . .).

-s	Transpose the rows and columns of output:
	
	```→ paste -s letters numbers```
	```A B C```
	```1 2 3 4 5```

File Text Manipulation | 87

```
tr [options] charset1 [charset2]
```

The tr command (short for "translate") performs some simple, useful translations of one set of characters into another. For example, to capitalize the text of a file:

```
→ cat myfile
This is a very wonderful file.
→ cat myfile | tr 'a-z' 'A-Z'
THIS IS A VERY WONDERFUL FILE.
```

or to change all vowels into asterisks:

```
→ cat myfile | tr aeiouAEIOU '*'
Th*s *s * v*ry w*nd*rf*l f*l*.
```

or to delete all vowels:

```
→ cat myfile | tr -d aeiouAEIOU
Ths s  vry wndrfl fl.
```

As a very practical example, delete all carriage returns from a DOS text file so it's more compatible with Terminal text utilities like grep:

```
→ tr -d '\r' < dosfile > newfile
```

tr translates the first character in *charset1* into the first character in *charset2*, the second into the second, the third into the third, etc. If the length of *charset1* is N, only the first N characters in *charset2* are used. If *charset1* is longer than *charset2*, the final character in *charset2* will be used repeatedly.

Character sets can have the following forms:

Form	Meaning
ABCD	The sequence of characters A, B, C, D.
A-B	The range of characters from A to B.
[x*y]	y repetitions of the character x.
[:*class*:]	The same character classes accepted by grep, such as [:alnum:], [:digit:], etc.

tr also understands the escape characters "\a" (^G = ring bell), "\b" (^H = backspace), "\f" (^L = formfeed), "\n" (^J = newline), "\r"

(^M = return), "\t" (^I = Tab), and "\v" (^K = vertical Tab) accepted by printf (see "Screen Output" on page 170), as well as the notation \nnn to mean the character with octal value nnn.

tr is great for quick and simple translations, but for more powerful jobs consider sed, awk, or perl.

Useful options

-d Delete the characters in *charset1* from the input.

-s Eliminate adjacent duplicates (found in *charset1*) from the input. For example, tr -s aeiouAEIOU would squeeze adjacent, duplicate vowels to be single vowels (reeeeeeally would become really).

-c Operate on all characters *not* found in *charset1*.

---

sort   stdin   stdout   - file   -- opt   --help   --version

sort [*options*] [*files*]

The sort command prints lines of text in alphabetical order, or sorted by some other rule you specify. All provided files are concatenated, and the result is sorted and printed:

```
→ cat myfile
def
xyz
abc
→ sort myfile
abc
def
xyz
```

Useful options

-f Case-insensitive sorting.

-n Sort numerically (i.e., 9 comes before 10) instead of alphabetically (10 comes before 9 because it begins with a "1").

-g Another numerical sorting method with a different algorithm that, among other things, recognizes scientific notation (7.4e3 means "7.4 times ten to the third power," or 7,400). Run info sort for full technical details.

-u	Unique sort: remove duplicate lines. (If used with -c for checking sorted files, fail if any consecutive lines are identical.)
-c	Don't sort, just check if the input is already sorted. If it is, print nothing; otherwise, print an error message.
-b	Ignore leading whitespace in lines.
-r	Reverse the output: sort from greatest to least.
-t X	Use X as the field delimiter for the -k option.
-k key	Choose sorting keys. (Combine with -t to choose a separator character between keys.)

A sorting key is a portion of a line that's considered when sorting, instead of considering the entire line. An example is "the fifth character of each line." Normally, **sort** would consider these lines to be in sorted order:

```
aaaaz
bbbby
```

but if your sorting key is "the fifth character of each line," then the lines are reversed because y comes before z. A more practical example involves this file of names and addresses:

```
→ cat people
George Washington,123 Main Street,New York
Abraham Lincoln,54 First Avenue,San Francisco
John Adams,39 Tremont Street,Boston
```

An ordinary sort would display the "Abraham Lincoln" line first. But if you consider each line as three comma-separated values, you can sort on the second value with:

```
→ sort -k2 -t, people
George Washington,123 Main Street,New York
John Adams,39 Tremont Street,Boston
Abraham Lincoln,54 First Avenue,San Francisco
```

where "123 Main Street" is first alphabetically. Likewise, you can sort on the city (third value) with:

```
→ sort -k3 -t, people
John Adams,39 Tremont Street,Boston
George Washington,123 Main Street,New York
Abraham Lincoln,54 First Avenue,San Francisco
```

and see that Boston comes up first alphabetically. The general syntax -k F1[.C1][,F2[.C2]] means:

Item	Meaning	Default if not supplied
F1	Starting field	Required
C1	Starting position within field 1	1
F2	Ending field	Last field
C2	Starting position within ending field	1

So sort -k1.5 sorts based on the first field, beginning at its fifth character; and sort -k2.8,5 means "from the eighth character of the second field to the first character of the fifth field." The -t option changes the behavior of -k so it considers delimiter characters such as commas rather than spaces.

You can repeat the -k option to define multiple keys, which will be applied from first to last as found on the command line.

---

uniq

stdin   stdout   - file   **-- opt**   --help   --version

uniq [options] [files]

The uniq command operates on consecutive, duplicate lines of text. For example, if you have a file *myfile*:

```
→ cat myfile
a
b
b
c
b
```

then uniq would detect and process (in whatever way you specify) the two consecutive b's, but not the third b:

```
→ uniq myfile
a
b
c
b
```

The input you send to uniq must have duplicate items next to each other, or uniq will have no effect. It's common to pipe the output of sort into uniq:

```
→ sort myfile | uniq
a
b
c
```

In this case, only a single b remains because all three were made adjacent by sort, then collapsed to one by uniq. Also, you can count duplicate lines instead of eliminating them:

```
→ sort myfile | uniq -c
      1 a
      3 b
      1 c
```

Useful options

- -c   Count adjacent duplicate lines.

- -i   Case-insensitive operation.

- -u   Print unique lines only.

- -d   Print duplicate lines only.

- -s *N* Ignore the first *N* characters on each line when detecting duplicates.

- -f *N* Ignore the first *N* whitespace-separated fields on each line when detecting duplicates.

---

tee   stdin   stdout   -file   --opt   --help   --version

```
tee [options] files
```

Like the cat command, the tee command copies standard input to standard output unaltered. Simultaneously, however, it also copies that same standard input to one or more files. tee is most often found in the middle of pipelines, writing some intermediate data to a file while also passing it to the next command in the pipeline:

```
→ who | tee original_who | sort
```

In this command line, tee writes the output of who to the file original_who, and then passes along that same output to the rest of the pipeline (sort), producing sorted output on screen.

Useful options

- `-a` Append instead of overwriting files.
- `-i` Ignore interrupt signals.

More Powerful Manipulations

We've just barely scratched the surface of text filtering. Terminal has hundreds of filters that produce ever more complex manipulations of the data. But with great power comes a great learning curve, too much for a short book. Here are a few filters to get you started.

awk

awk is a pattern-matching language. It matches data by regular expression and then performs actions based on the data. Here are a few simple examples for processing a text file, *myfile*.

Print the second and fourth word on each line:

```
→ awk '{print $2, $4}' myfile
```

Print all lines that are shorter than 60 characters:

```
→ awk 'length < 60 {print}' myfile
```

sed

Like awk, sed is a pattern-matching engine that can perform manipulations on lines of text. Its syntax is closely related to that of vim and the line editor ed. Here are some trivial examples.

Print the file with all occurrences of the string "PC" changed to "Mac":

```
→ sed 's/PC/Mac/g' myfile
```

Print the file with the first 10 lines removed:

```
→ sed '1,10d' myfile
```

Perl, PHP, Python

Perl, PHP, and Python are full-fledged scripting languages powerful enough to build complete, robust applications. See "Beyond Shell Scripting" on page 208 for references.

File Location

find   Locate files in a directory hierarchy.

xargs   Process a list of located files (and much more).

locate   Create an index of files, and search the index for string.

which   Locate executables in your search path (command).

type   Locate executables in your search path (bash built-in).

whereis   Locate executables, documentation, and source files.

A Macintosh can contain hundreds of thousands of files easily. How can you find a particular file when you need to? The first step is to organize your files logically into directories in some thoughtful manner, but there are several other ways to find files, including those that the Finder's built-in search cannot locate.

For finding any file, **find** is a brute-force program that slogs file-by-file through a directory hierarchy to locate a target. **locate** is much faster, searching through a prebuilt index that you generate as needed. OS X does not generate the index by default, but you can set it up to do so.

For finding programs, the **which** and **type** commands check all directories in your shell search path. **type** is built into the bash shell, while **which** is a program (normally *usr/bin/which*); **type** is faster and can detect shell aliases. In contrast, **whereis** examines a known set of directories, rather than your search path.

---

find   stdin **stdout** - file -- opt --help --version

find [*directories*] [*expression*]

The find command searches one or more directories (and their subdirectories recursively) for files matching certain criteria. It is very powerful, with over 50 options and, unfortunately, a rather

---

unusual syntax. Here are some simple examples that search the entire filesystem from the root directory:

Find a particular file named *myfile*:

   → `find / -type f -name myfile -print`

Print all directory names:

   → `find / -type d -print`

Print filenames ending in ".txt" (notice how the wildcard is escaped so the shell ignores it):

   → `find / -type f -name \*.txt -print`

Useful options

`-name pattern` `-path pattern` `-lname pattern`	The name (-name), pathname (-path), or symbolic link target (-lname) of the desired file must match this shell pattern, which may include shell wildcards *, ?, and []. (You must escape the wildcards, however, so they are ignored by the shell and passed literally to find.) Paths are relative to the directory tree being searched.
`-iname pattern` `-ipath pattern` `-ilname pattern`	The -iname, -ipath and -ilname options are the same as -name, -path, and -lname, respectively, but are case-insensitive. (Even though the OS X filesystem is case-insensitive, the find command is case-sensitive when it matches filenames.)
`-regex regexp`	The path (relative to the directory tree being searched) must match the given regular expression.
`-type t`	Locate only files of type t. This includes plain files (f), directories (d), symbolic links (l), block devices (b), character devices (c), named pipes (p), and sockets (s).
`-atime N` `-ctime N` `-mtime N`	File was last accessed (-atime), last modified (-mtime), or had a status change (-ctime) exactly $N*24$ hours ago. Use $+N$ for "greater than N," or $-N$ for "less than N."
`-amin N` `-cmin N` `-mmin N`	File was last accessed (-amin), last modified (-mmin), or had a status change (-cmin) exactly N minutes ago. Use $+N$ for "greater than N," or $-N$ for "less than N."

-anewer *other_file* -cnewer *other_file* -newer *other_file*	File was accessed (-anewer), modified (-newer), or had a status change (-cnewer) more recently than *other_file* has.
-maxdepth *N* -mindepth *N*	Consider files at least (-mindepth) or at most (-maxdepth) *N* levels deep in the directory tree being searched.
-L	Follow symbolic links, using attributes of the destination file instead of the link.
-x	Limit the search to a single filesystem, i.e., don't cross device boundaries.
-size *N* [bckw]	Consider files of size *N*, which can be given in blocks (b), one-byte characters (c), kilobytes (k), or two-byte words (w). Use +*N* for "greater than *N*," or -*N* for "less than *N*."
-empty	File has zero size, and is a regular file or directory.
-user *name*	File is owned by the given user.
-group *name*	File is owned by the given group.
-perm *mode*	File has permissions equal to *mode*. Use - *mode* to check that *all* of the given bits are set, or +*mode* to check that *any* of the given bits are set.

You can group and negate parts of the expression with the following operators:

expression1 -and *expression2*
> And. (This is the default if two expressions appear side by side, so the "-and" is optional.)

expression1 -or *expression2*
> Or.

! *expression*
-not *expression*
> Negate the expression.

(*expression*)
> Precedence markers, just like in algebra class. Evaluate what's in parentheses first. You may need to escape these from the shell with "\".

Once you've specified the search criteria, you can tell find to perform these actions on files that match the criteria.

Useful options

-print
: Simply print the path to the file, relative to the search directory.

-print0
: Like -print, but instead of separating each line of output with a newline character, use a null (ASCII 0) character. Use when piping the output of find to another program, and your list of filenames may contain space characters. Of course, the receiving program must be capable of reading and parsing these null-separated lines—for example, xargs -0.

-exec *cmd* ;
: Invoke the given shell command, *cmd*. Make sure to escape any shell metacharacters, including the required, final semicolon, so they are not immediately evaluated on the command line. Also, the symbol "{}" (make sure to quote or escape it) represents the path to the file found.

-ok *cmd* ;
: Same as -exec, but also prompts the user before invoking each command.

-ls
: Perform the command ls -dils on the file.

---

xargs stdin stdout -file --opt --help --version

xargs [*options*] [*command*]

xargs is one of the oddest yet most powerful commands available to the shell. It reads lines of text from standard input, turns them into commands, and executes them. This might not sound exciting, but xargs has some unique uses, particularly for processing a list of files you've located. Suppose you made a file named *important* that lists important files, one per line:

```
→ cat important
/Users/jsmith/mail/love-letters
/usr/local/lib/critical_stuff
/etc/passwd
...
```

With `xargs`, you can process each of these files easily with other commands. For instance, the following command runs the `ls -l` command on all the listed files:

→ `cat important | xargs ls -l`

Similarly, you can view the files with `less`:

→ `cat important | xargs less`

and even delete them with `rm` (but be careful, because they'll be destroyed without any warnings):

→ `cat important | xargs rm`   *Warning! Deletes files!*

Each of these pipelines reads the list of files from *important* and produces and runs new commands based on the list. The power begins when the input list doesn't come from a file, but from another command writing to standard output. In particular, the `find` command, which prints a list of files on standard output, makes a great partner for `xargs`. For example, to search your current directory hierarchy for files containing the word "myxomatosis":

→ `find . -print | xargs grep -l myxomatosis`

This power comes with one warning: if any of the files located by `find` contains whitespace in its name, this will confuse `grep`. If one file is named (say) *my stuff*, then the `grep` command constructed is:

→ `grep -l myxomatosis my stuff`

which tells `grep` to process *two* files named *my* and *stuff*. Oops! Now imagine if the program had been `rm` instead of `grep`. You'd be telling `rm` to delete the wrong files! To avoid this problem with `xargs`:

1. Always use `find -print0` instead of `-print`, which separates lines with ASCII null characters instead of newline characters.

2. Combine this with `xargs -0`, which expects ASCII nulls.

As an example:

→ `find . -print0 | xargs -0 grep -l myxomatosis`

We have barely scratched the surface of the `xargs` command, so please experiment! (With harmless commands like `grep` and `ls` at first!)

Useful options

- **-n** *k* Feed *k* lines of input to the command being executed. A common scenario is to use -n1, guaranteeing that each execution will process only one line of input. Otherwise, xargs may pass multiple lines of input to a single command.

- **-0** Set the end-of-line character for input to be ASCII zero rather than whitespace, and treat all characters literally. Use this when the input is coming from find -print0.

---

xargs Versus Backquotes

If you remember "Quoting" on page 34, you might realize that some xargs tricks can be accomplished with backquotes. Here we delete a list of files whose names are in *file_list*, one per line. (Be careful: files will be deleted without any warning.)

```
→ cat file_list | xargs rm -f      with xargs
→ rm -f `cat file_list`            with backquotes
```

While both commands do similar things, backquotes can fail if the command line gets so long, after the quoted part is expanded, that it exceeds the maximum length of a shell command line. xargs does not have this limitation, so it's safer and more suitable for large or risky operations.

---

locate

stdin **stdout** - file -- opt --help --version

```
locate [options]
```

The locate command searches an index (database) of file locations to locate a given file. If you plan to locate many files over time in a directory hierarchy that doesn't change much, locate is a good choice. For locating a single file or performing more complex processing of found files, use find.

You can set up OS X to index the entire filesystem on a regular basis (e.g., once a day), meaning you can simply run locate and it will work. To do this, run:

```
→ sudo launchctl load -w \
  /System/Library/LaunchDaemons/com.apple.locate.plist
```

This starts generating the index, which may take a while to complete.[10] Then you can locate files by name with:

→ `locate myfile`

At this point, you might wonder why `locate` is necessary, since every Finder window has a Search box for locating files. In fact, this Finder feature does not locate system files that are normally hidden by the Finder. Try searching with the Finder for `who`, for instance, and it will not locate `/usr/bin/who`.[11]

Useful options

-i   Case-insensitive search.

-l N   Display only the first N files.

---

which   stdin **stdout** - file **-- opt** --help --version

`which file`

The `which` command locates an executable file in your shell's search path. If you've been invoking a program by typing its name:

→ `who`

the `which` command tells you where this command is located:

→ `which who`
`/usr/bin/who`

You can even find the `which` program itself:

→ `which which`
`/usr/bin/which`

---

10. The `launchctl` command is covered in "Scheduling Jobs" on page 130.
11. You can make the Finder search for system files with a bit of work. Perform a search, then click the + button and look for the Kind dropdown. Change it to Other, then select System Files, click OK, and then change "aren't included" to "are included." Now you can search for system files in the Finder, but only in that Finder window. Once you close it, you have to do the preceding steps all over again. Ugh.

If several programs in your search path have the same name (for example, *usr/bin/who* and *usr/local/bin/who*), which reports only the first.

---

type

type [*options*] *commands*

The type command, like which, locates an executable file in your shell's search path:

```
→ type cat who
cat is /bin/cat
who is /usr/bin/who
```

However, type is built into the bash shell, whereas which is a program on disk. The type command reveals this:

```
→ type which type
which is /usr/bin/which
type is a shell builtin
```

as well as the locations of other commands:

```
→ type rm if
rm is aliased to `/bin/rm -i'
if is a shell keyword
```

As a built-in command, type is faster than which; however, it's available only if your shell is bash.

---

whereis

whereis *programs*

The whereis command attempts to locate executable programs by searching a predetermined list of directories. It operates like which but may also check directories outside of your search path:

```
→ whereis locate
/usr/bin/locate
```

File Compression and Packaging

`gzip`	Compress files with GNU Zip.
`gunzip`	Uncompress GNU Zip files.
`bzip2`	Compress files in BZip format.
`bunzip2`	Uncompress BZip files.
`bzcat`	Compress/uncompress BZip files via standard input/output.
`compress`	Compress files with traditional Unix compression.
`uncompress`	Uncompress files with traditional Unix compression.
`zcat`	Compress/uncompress file via standard input/output (gzip or compress).
`zip`	Compress files in Windows Zip format.
`unzip`	Uncompress Windows Zip files.
`tar`	Package multiple files into a single file.

The Terminal has commands to compress files into a variety of formats and uncompress them. The most popular formats are GNU Zip (**gzip**), whose compressed files are named with the *.gz* suffix, and BZip, which uses the *.bz2* suffix. Other common formats include Zip files from Windows systems (*.zip* suffix) and occasionally, classic Unix compression (*.Z* suffix).

If you come across a format we don't cover, such as Macintosh *sit* files, Arc, Zoo, *rar*, and others, you can head over to *http://en.wikipedia.org/wiki/List_of_archive_formats* to learn more.

---

gzip   stdin   stdout   - file   -- opt   --help   --version

`gzip [options] [files]`

The `gzip`, `gunzip`, and `zcat` commands compress and uncompress files in GNU Zip format. Compressed files have the suffix *.gz*.

Sample commands

gzip *file*	Compress *file* to create *file.gz*. Original *file* is deleted.
gzip -c *file*	Produce compressed data on standard output.
cat *file* | gzip	Produce compressed data from a pipeline.
gunzip *file.gz*	Uncompress *file.gz* to create *file*. Original *file.gz* is deleted.
gunzip -c *file.gz*	Uncompress the data on standard output.
cat *file.gz* | gunzip	Uncompress the data from a pipeline.
zcat *file.gz*	Uncompress the data on standard output.

---

bzip2   stdin stdout - file -- opt --help --version

bzip2 [*options*] [*files*]

The bzip2, bunzip2, and bzcat commands compress and uncompress files in Burrows-Wheeler format. Compressed files have the suffix *.bz2*.

Sample commands

bzip2 *file*	Compress *file* to create *file.bz2*. Original *file* is deleted.
bzip2 -c *file*	Produce compressed data on standard output.
cat *file* | bzip2	Produce compressed data from a pipeline.
bunzip2 *file.bz2*	Uncompress *file.bz2* to create *file*. Original *file.bz2* is deleted.
bunzip2 -c *file.bz2*	Uncompress the data on standard output.
cat *file.bz2* | bunzip2	Uncompress the data from a pipeline.
bzcat *file.bz2*	Uncompress the data on standard output.

compress

stdin   stdout   - file   -- opt   --help   --version

compress [*options*] [*files*]

The compress and uncompress commands compress and uncompress files in standard Unix compression format (Lempel Ziv). Compressed files have the suffix .Z.

Sample commands

compress *file*	Compress *file* to create *file.Z*. Original *file* is deleted.
compress -c *file*	Produce compressed data on standard output.
cat *file* | compress	Produce compressed data from a pipeline.
uncompress *file.Z*	Uncompress *file.Z* to create *file*. Original *file.Z* is deleted.
uncompress -c *file.Z*	Uncompress the data on standard output.
cat *file.Z* | uncompress	Uncompress the data from a pipeline.
zcat *file.Z*	Uncompress the data on standard output.

zip

stdin   stdout   - file   -- opt   **--help**   **--version**

zip [*options*] [*files*]

The zip and unzip commands compress and uncompress files in Windows Zip format. Compressed files have the suffix .*zip*. Unlike the preceding compression commands, zip does not delete the original files.

zip *myfile.zip file1 file2 file3* ...	Pack.
zip -r *myfile.zip dirname*	Pack recursively.
unzip -l *myfile.zip*	List contents.
unzip *myfile* .zip	Unpack.

tar [*options*] [*files*]

The tar program packs multiple files and directories into a single archive file for transport. Originally for backing up files onto a tape drive (its name is short for "tape archive"), tar is still a common file-packaging format. Using various options, you can create archive files, list their contents, and extract the files:

> → tar -cvf myarchive.tar mydir   *Create*
> → tar -tvf myarchive.tar   *List contents*
> → tar -xvf myarchive.tar   *Extract*

It's your responsibility to name the archive file properly; tar will not add a *.tar* suffix for you. TAR files are usually compressed with the other programs we covered in this section. Here are sample commands for archiving a directory *mydir* when compressed with gzip:

> → tar -czvf myarchive.tar.gz mydir   *Create archive*
> → tar -tzvf myarchive.tar.gz   *List contents*
> → tar -xzvf myarchive.tar.gz   *Extract*

or compressed with bzip2:

> → tar -cjvf myarchive.tar.bz2 mydir   *Create archive*
> → tar -tjvf myarchive.tar.bz2   *List contents*
> → tar -xjvf myarchive.tar.bz2   *Extract*

or compressed with compress:

> → tar -cZvf myarchive.tar.Z mydir   *Create archive*
> → tar -tZvf myarchive.tar.Z   *List contents*
> → tar -xZvf myarchive.tar.Z   *Extract*

If you specify files on the command line, only those files are processed. To extract *file1*, *file2*, and *file3* from a TAR file *myarchive.tar*, run:

> → tar -xvf myarchive.tar file1 file2 file3

Otherwise, the entire archive is processed.

Useful options

-c   Create an archive. You'll have to list the input files and directories on the command line.

`-r`	Append files to an existing archive.
`-u`	Append new/changed files to an existing archive.
`-t`	List the archive.
`-x`	Extract files from the archive.
`-f file`	Read the archive from, or write the archive to, the given file. This is usually a TAR file on disk (such as *myarchive.tar*) but can also be a tape drive (such as */dev/st0*).
`-z`	Use `gzip` compression.
`-j`	Use `bzip2` compression.
`-Z`	Use Unix compression.
`-b N`	Use a block size of *N* * 512 bytes.
`-v`	Verbose mode: print extra information.
`-h`	Follow symbolic links rather than merely copying them.
`-p`	When extracting files, restore their original permissions and ownership.

File Comparison

`diff`	Line-by-line comparison of two files or directories.
`comm`	Line-by-line comparison of two sorted files.
`cmp`	Byte-by-byte comparison of two files.
`md5`	Compute a checksum of the given files.

There are three ways to compare files:

- Line by line (**diff**, **comm**), best suited to text files
- Byte by byte (**cmp**), often used for binary files
- By comparing checksums (**md5**)

These programs are all text-based. For a graphical file-comparison tool, try **xxdiff** at *http://furius.ca/xxdiff*.

```
diff [options] file1 file2
```

The diff command compares two files line by line, or two directories. When comparing text files, diff can produce detailed reports of their differences. For binary files, diff merely reports whether they differ or not. For all files, if there are no differences, diff produces no output.

The traditional output format looks like this:

> *Indication of line numbers and the type of change*
> < *Corresponding section of file1, if any*
> ---
> > *Corresponding section of file2, if any*

For example, if we start with a file *fileA*:

```
Hello, this is a wonderful file.
The quick brown fox jumped over
the lazy dogs.
Goodbye for now.
```

Suppose we delete the first line, change "brown" to "blue" on the second line, and add a final line, creating a file *fileB*:

```
The quick blue fox jumped over
the lazy dogs.
Goodbye for now.
Macs r00l!
```

Then diff fileA fileB produces this output:

```
1,2c1                              fileA lines 1–2 became fileB line 1
< Hello, this is a wonderful file. Lines 1–2 of fileA
< The quick brown fox jumped over
---                                diff separator
> The quick blue fox jumped over   Line 1 of fileB

4a4                                Line 4 was added in fileB
> Macs r00l!                       The added line
```

The leading symbols < and > are arrows indicating *fileA* and *fileB*, respectively. This output format is the default: many others are available, some of which can be fed directly to other tools. Try them out to see what they look like.

Option	Output format
-n	RCS version control format, as produced by the command `rcsdiff` (man `rcsdiff`).
-c	Context diff format, as used by the `patch` command (man `patch`).
-D *macro*	C preprocessor format, using `#ifdef` *macro* ... `#else` ... `#endif`.
-u	Unified format, which merges the files and prepends "-" for deletion and "+" for addition.
-y	Side-by-side format; use -W to adjust the width of the output.
-e	Create an ed script that would change *fileA* into *fileB* if run.
-q	Don't report changes, just say whether the files differ.

`diff` can also compare directories:

> → `diff dir1 dir2`

which compares any same-named files in those directories, and lists all files that appear in one directory but not the other. To compare entire directory hierarchies recursively, use the -r option:

> → `diff -r dir1 dir2`

which produces a (potentially massive) report of all differences.

Useful options

- -b Don't consider whitespace.
- -B Don't consider blank lines.
- -i Case-insensitive operation.
- -r When comparing directories, recurse into subdirectories.

`diff` is just one member of a family of programs that operate on file differences. Some others are `diff3`, which compares three files at a time, and `sdiff`, which merges the differences between two files to create a third file according to your instructions.

```
comm [options] file1 file2
```

The comm command compares two sorted files and produces three columns of output, separated by tabs:

1. All lines that appear in *file1* but not in *file2*.

2. All lines that appear in *file2* but not in *file1*.

3. All lines that appear in both files.

For example, if *file1* and *file2* contain these lines:

file1:	*file2:*
apple	baker
baker	charlie
charlie	dark

then comm produces this three-column output:

```
→ comm file1 file2
apple
                baker
                charlie
        dark
```

Useful options

- -1   Suppress column 1.

- -2   Suppress column 2.

- -3   Suppress column 3.

- -i   Case-insensitive operation.

---

cmp   stdin   stdout   - file   -- opt   --help   --version

```
cmp [options] file1 file2 [offset1 [offset2]]
```

The cmp command compares two files. If their contents are the same, cmp reports nothing; otherwise, it lists the location of the first difference:

```
→ cmp myfile yourfile
myfile yourfile differ: char 494, line 17
```

By default, cmp does not tell you what the difference is, only where it is. It also is perfectly suitable for comparing binary files, as opposed to diff, which operates best on text files.

Normally, cmp starts its comparison at the beginning of each file, but it will start elsewhere if you provide offsets:

→ `cmp myfile yourfile 10 20`

This begins the comparison at the tenth byte of *myfile* and the twentieth of *yourfile*.

Useful options

-l   Long output: print all differences, byte by byte:

→ `cmp -l myfile yourfile`
`494 164 172`

This means at offset 494 (in decimal), *myfile* has "t" (octal 164) but *yourfile* has "z" (octal 172).

-s   Silent output: don't print anything, just exit with an appropriate return code; 0 if the files match, 1 if they don't. (Or other codes if the comparison fails for some reason.)

---

md5   **stdin**   **stdout**   - file   **-- opt**   --help   --version

`md5 files`

The md5 command does not compare files, but it does something related: it computes and displays checksums of files to verify that the files are unchanged. It produces 32-byte checksums using the MD5 algorithm:

→ `md5 myfile`
`MD5 (myfile) = d3b07384d113edec49eaa6238ad5ff00`

If one file differs even slightly from another file, the two files are highly unlikely to have the same MD5 checksum, so comparing checksums is a reasonably reliable way to detect if two files differ. Here we write two checksums to two files (piping through cut to extract the checksum value after the equals sign) and compare them:

```
→ md5 myfile1 | cut -d= -f2 > sum1
→ md5 myfile2 | cut -d= -f2 > sum2
→ diff -q sum1 sum2
Files sum1 and sum2 differ
→ rm sum1 sum2                          Clean up
```

When a very large file is available for download on the Internet, such as a disk image, its creator often publishes the checksum. When you download such a file, you can compute the checksum locally and compare it easily to the published one, verifying that the large file was not corrupted during transmission:

```
→ md5 diskfile.iso > mine.md5
→ diff -q original.md5 mine.md5
```

Some other programs similar to md5 are sum and cksum, which use different algorithms to compute their checksums. sum is compatible with Unix systems, specifically BSD Unix (the default) or System V Unix (-s option), and cksum produces a CRC checksum:

```
→ sum myfile
12410  3   myfile
→ cksum myfile
1204834076  2863   myfile
```

The first integer is a checksum and the second is a block count. But as you can see, these checksums are small numbers and therefore unreliable, since files could have identical checksums by coincidence. md5 is by far the best. See *http://www.faqs.org/rfcs/rfc1321.html* for the technical details.

Printing

lpr   Print a file.

lpq   View the print queue.

lprm   Remove a print job from the queue.

You can print directly from the command line using the **lpr** family of commands. Well...sort of. Out of the box, these commands work fine for plain text and PostScript files, but not for documents like spreadsheets or Photoshop images. For those, you'll need to run the document's application (e.g., Photoshop) and use its Print command.

---

lpr

`lpr [options] [files]`

The lpr (line printer) command sends a file to a printer. To print on your default printer (or if you have just a single printer set up), run:

→ `lpr myfile.txt`

If your Mac is set up with multiple printers, then to print on a different printer than the default, supply the name of the printer with the -P option:

→ `lpr -P myprinter myfile.txt`

The names of your printers can be listed with the lpstat command:

→ `lpstat -p`
`printer HP_Color_LaserJet_2605dn is idle.`
`enabled since Tue Apr 24 21:00:42 2012`

Now to print on this printer, run:

→ `lpr -P HP_Color_LaserJet_2605dn myfile`

Useful options

-P *printername*	Send the file to printer *printername*, which you have set up previously.
-# *N*	Print *N* copies of the file.
-J *name*	Set the job *name* that prints on the cover page (if your system is set up to print cover pages).

---

lpq

`lpq [options]`

The lpq (line printer queue) command lists all print jobs waiting to be printed.

```
→ lpq
HP_Color_LaserJet_2605dn is ready and printing
Rank    Owner   Job   File(s)        Total Size
active  (null)  1     untitled       1024 bytes
```

Useful options

-P *printername*	List the queue for printer *printername*.
-a	List the queue for all printers.
-l	Be verbose: display information in a longer format.

---

lprm   stdin   **stdout**   - file   -- opt   --help   --version

lprm [*options*] [*job_IDs*]

The lprm (line printer remove) command cancels one or more print jobs. Use lpq to learn the ID of the desired print jobs (say, 61 and 78), then type:

→ **lprm -P** *printername* **61 78**

If you don't supply any job IDs, your current print job is canceled. (Only the superuser can cancel other users' jobs.) The -P option specifies which print queue to process.

Disks and Filesystems

df	Display available space on mounted filesystems.
diskutil	Perform operations on disks and partitions: mounting, formatting, re-naming, and more.
mount	Mount remote (or local) disks and partitions.
fsck_hfs	Check a Macintosh HFS disk partition for errors.
hdiutil	Work with disk images, such as ISO and DMG files.
tmutil	Perform Time Machine operations.
sync	Flush all disk caches to disk.
rsync	Mirror a set of files onto another device or host.

Macs can have multiple disks or disk partitions. In casual conversation, these are variously called disks, partitions, filesystems, volumes, even directories. We'll try to be more accurate.

A *disk* is a hardware device, which may be divided into *partitions* that act as independent storage devices. You might think of disks and partitions as icons on the desktop or in the */Volumes* folder, but in fact OS X represents them as special files in the directory */dev*. For example, a typical Mac could have its system disk partition on */dev/disk0s2*, a DVD drive on */dev/disk1*, and an ancient SCSI tape drive on */dev/st0*.

Before a partition can hold files, it is "formatted" by a program that writes a *filesystem* on it. A filesystem defines how files are represented; examples are HFS Plus (the traditional OS X filesystem) and NTFS (Microsoft Windows NT filesystem). Formatting is done by applications like Disk Utility, in the Mac's *Utilities* folder. We will examine several command-line tools that do disk operations.

Once a filesystem is created, you can make it available for use by *mounting* it on an empty directory. For example, if you mount a Windows filesystem on a directory */Volumes/win*, it becomes part of your system's directory tree, and you can create and edit files like */Volumes/win/myfile*. Mounting is generally done automatically, either at boot time or upon attaching a portable drive. Filesystems can also be unmounted to make them inaccessible, say, for maintenance.

---

df

stdin   **stdout**   - file   **-- opt**   --help   --version

df [`options`] [`disk devices | files | directories`]

The df (disk free) program shows you the size, used space, and free space on a given disk partition. If you supply a file or directory, df describes the disk device on which that file or directory resides. With no arguments, df reports on all mounted filesystems. Here we use the -h option to display in sizes in rounded kilobytes (Ki), gigabytes (Gi), and terabytes (Ti):

```
→ df -h
Filesystem    Size   Used  Avail Capacity Mounted on
/dev/disk0s2  111Gi  21Gi  90Gi    20%    /
devfs         107Ki  107Ki  0      100%   /dev
/dev/disk1s2  1.8Ti  84Gi  1.7Ti    5%    /Volumes/Music
...
```

Useful options

-b	List sizes in 512-byte blocks (the default).
-k	List sizes in kilobytes.
-m	List sizes in megabytes.
-h -H	Print human-readable output, and choose the most appropriate unit for each size. For example, if your two disks have 1 gigabyte and 25 kilobytes free, respectively, df -h prints 1G and 25K. The -h option uses powers of 1024, whereas -H uses powers of 1000.
-l	Display only local filesystems, not networked filesystems.
-T type	Display only filesystems of the given type.
-i	Inode mode. Display total, used, and free inodes for each filesystem, instead of disk blocks.

---

diskutil   stdin   **stdout**   -file   --opt   --help   --version

```
diskutil action [options]
```

The diskutil command operates on disk partitions: mounting and unmounting, getting information, renaming, erasing, and more. Read-only operations can be done by any user, but writing and mounting require an administrator. For example, if you have a portable USB drive mounted:

```
→ df -h /Volumes/MyUSB
Filesystem    Size   Used  Avail Capacity Mounted on
/dev/disk1s2  1.8Ti  813Mi 1.8Ti   1%     /Volumes/MyUSB
```

you can unmount it with either of these diskutil commands, by providing the directory where it's mounted:

```
→ sudo diskutil unmount /Volumes/MyUSB
Volume MyUSB on disk1s2 unmounted
```

or the associated device in the *dev* directory:

```
→ sudo diskutil unmount /dev/disk1s2
Volume MyUSB on disk1s2 unmounted
```

and since it's a portable drive, even eject it for safe unplugging from the Mac:

```
→ sudo diskutil eject /dev/disk1s2
Disk /dev/disk1s2 ejected
```

Then you can remount it by its device name:

```
→ sudo diskutil mount /dev/disk1s2
Volume MyUSB on /dev/disk1s2 mounted
```

diskutil does many other tricks, such as getting information about a partition:

```
→ diskutil info /Volumes/MyUSB
Device Node:      /dev/disk1s2
File System:      HFS+
Name:             Mac OS Extended
Bootable:         Is bootable
Protocol:         USB
Total Size:       2.0 TB (2000054960128 Bytes)
Ejectable:        Yes
...
```

renaming a partition:

```
→ sudo diskutil rename /dev/disk1s2 OtherName
Volume on disk1s2 renamed to OtherName
```

and checking its internal structure for errors:[12]

```
→ sudo diskutil verifyVolume /dev/disk1s2
Started filesystem verification on disk1s2 MyUSB
Checking Journaled HFS Plus volume
Checking extents overflow file
...
```

You can also reformat (erase) a partition, but *be careful*: the operation begins immediately with no questions or warnings! First, find out what types of filesystems can be written on the disk:

```
→ diskutil listFilesystems
PERSONALITY                     USER VISIBLE NAME
-------------------------------------------------
ExFAT                           ExFAT
```

12. Or run the program fsck_hfs, which does the same thing.

```
MS-DOS FAT32                    MS-DOS (FAT32)
HFS+                           Mac OS Extended
...
```

Then provide your desired filesystem type and a name for the partition, such as CoolDisk, and erase it:[13]

```
→ sudo diskutil erase HFS+ CoolDisk /dev/disk1s2
Started erase on disk1s2 CoolDisk ...
```

There are many more operations supported with various options: repartitioning a drive, erasing an entire drive, repairing errors, controlling HFS journaling, and more. See the manpage for full information.

One final note: if you come from a Linux background, you might be accustomed to the programs mount and umount for disk partitions. These commands are available in OS X, but use diskutil whenever possible. It can be more reliable in some situations "due to the complex and interwoven nature of Mac OS X" (from the manpage for umount).

---

mount   stdin   stdout   -file   --opt   --help   --version

```
mount [options] partition dir
```

The mount command, like diskutil, makes a disk partition available and accessible on the Mac. Unlike diskutil, however, mount can work with remote systems such as Windows share drives or NFS. It has the same functionality as the Finder's "Connect to Server…" feature in the Go menu.

Suppose you have a Windows server, myserver, with a share named Work, and your login name on that server is jones. To mount the share on your Mac in a directory *mydir*, run:

```
→ mkdir mydir
→ mount -t smbfs //jones@myserver/Work mydir
Password: *******
```

---

13. After reformatting, OS X might display dialogs on the Mac desktop, so if you're logged in to the Mac remotely via SSH (discussed in "Running a Shell Remotely" on page 183), this might surprise whoever is using the desktop.

After you enter jones's password, the Windows share is mounted in *mydir*, ready for use:

```
→ ls mydir
file1.txt   file2.doc   ...
→ emacs mydir/file1.txt                    Edit a remote file
```

To unmount the Windows share, use the umount command:

```
→ umount mydir
```

If the same filesystem were served by NFS (Network File System) instead of a Windows share, the command would be:

```
→ mount -t nfs myserver:/Work mydir
```

Useful options

-t *type*	Declare that the mounted device has a particular filesystem type. Some common values are hfs for the Macintosh Hierarchical File System, ufs for UNIX filesystems (the default), smbfs for Microsoft Windows shares, and nfs for Network File System. For a complete list, list the directory */sbin* for programs whose names begin with *mount_*:

```
→ ls /sbin/mount_*
/sbin/mount_afp   /sbin/mount_cd9660   ...
```

Each suffix after *mount_* represents a value of -t.

-r	Mount the filesystem read-only.
-w	Mount the filesystem read-write.

---

fsck_hfs

stdin · **stdout** · - file · -- opt · --help · --version

```
fsck_hfs [options] [devices]
```

The fsck_hfs command validates a Macintosh HFS-formatted disk partition and, if requested, repairs errors found on it. (Alternatively, you can run the diskutil command, or the graphical application Disk Utility in the *Utilities* folder.) In general, unmount a device before checking it, so no other programs are operating on it at the same time:

```
→ sudo diskutil unmount /dev/disk1s2
→ sudo fsck_hfs -f /dev/disk1s2
** /dev/rdisk1s2
```

```
** Checking Journaled HFS Plus volume.
** Checking Extents Overflow file.
** Checking Catalog file.
** Checking multi-linked files.
...
```

OS X includes more validation programs for other kinds of filesystems. Run man -k fsck to see a list.

Useful options

- -f   Force a filesystem check, even if OS X says the filesystem doesn't need it.

- -n   Do not fix errors, just report them.

- -y   Fix errors automatically (use only if you *really* know what you're doing; if not, you can seriously mess up a filesystem).

---

hdiutil   stdin   stdout   -file   --opt   --help   --version

hdiutil *action* [*options*]

hdiutil works with disk images, such as ISO or DMG files downloaded from the Internet. You can mount, unmount, create, resize, verify, and even burn images onto discs. To mount an ISO file *mydisk.iso* as a volume and access its contents, run:

```
→ hdiutil attach mydisk.iso
→ ls /Volumes
MyDisk                    It's mounted in /Volumes
```

To unmount it when you're done, use the detach action, passing it the name of the mounted directory in */Volumes*:

```
→ hdiutil detach /Volumes/MyDisk
```

To check that the image is valid and undamaged, run:

```
→ hdiutil verify mydisk.iso
```

To burn the image to a CD or DVD, run:

```
→ hdiutil burn mydisk.iso
```

hdiutil has many other actions and dozens of options: see the manpage for details.

tmutil

`tmutil` *action* [*options*]

The `tmutil` command, introduced in OS X Lion, performs more than 20 actions with Time Machine, the Mac's backup software. For example, you can turn automatic backups on and off with:

→ **sudo tmutil enable**
→ **sudo tmutil disable**

turn local snapshots on and off with:

→ **sudo tmutil enablelocal**
→ **sudo tmutil disablelocal**

take a snapshot with:

→ **tmutil snapshot**

start a backup with:

→ **tmutil startbackup**

halt a backup with:

→ **tmutil stopbackup**

and list your backups with:

→ **tmutil stopbackup**

There are many other actions: see the manpage for details.

---

sync

sync

The `sync` command flushes all disk caches to disk. OS X usually buffers reads, writes, inode changes, and other disk-related activity in memory. `sync` writes the changes to disk. Normally, you don't need to run this command, but if, say, you're about to do something risky that might crash your machine, running `sync` immediately beforehand will make sure any pending disk writes are completed first.

rsync [*options*] *source destination*

The rsync command is perfect for copying large sets of files for backups. It is also very fast because it copies only the parts of files that have changed, rather than entire files. You might remember rsync from the beginning of the book, where it solved the problem of copying only changed files to a remote server.

rsync is not as simple as Apple's Time Machine, but it's very flexible, supports other platforms besides OS X, and can be controlled precisely from the command line. rsync can make an exact copy of all files, including file permissions and other attributes (called *mirroring*), or it can just copy the data. It can run over a network or on a single machine. It's also very fast compared to an ordinary copy command.

rsync has many uses and over 50 options; we'll present just a few common cases relating to backups.[14]

---

rsync and Extended Attributes

Always include the -E option when copying files to a Macintosh. This option ensures that OS X extended attributes and resource forks are copied. If the destination for your files is a Windows or Linux machine, -E is not important, since these other platforms do not store Mac extended attributes.

To mirror (copy exactly) the directory *D1* and its contents into another directory *D2* on a single machine:

→ rsync -a -E D1 D2

In order to mirror directory *D1* over the network to another host, *server.example.com*, where you have an account with username smith, secure the connection with SSH to prevent eavesdropping:

---

14. A related command is ditto, which copies files on a single Macintosh. rsync, in contrast, also runs on Windows, Linux, and other operating systems and can copy files over a network securely. See man ditto for more details.

→ `rsync -a -E -e ssh D1 smith@server.example.com:D2`

Useful options

-E	Copy Macintosh extended attributes and resource forks. Always include this option.
-o	Copy the ownership of the files. (You might need superuser privileges on the destination host.)
-g	Copy the group ownership of the files. (You might need superuser privileges on the destination host.)
-p	Copy the file permissions.
-t	Copy the file timestamps.
-r	Copy directories recursively, i.e., including their contents.
-l	Permit symbolic links to be copied (not the files they point to).
-D	Permit devices to be copied. (Superuser only.)
-a	Mirroring: copy all attributes of the original files. This implies the options -ogptrlD (but not -E).
-v	Verbose mode: print information about what's happening during the copy. Add --progress to display a numeric progress meter while files are copied.
-e ssh	Connect via ssh for more security. (Other remote shells are possible, but ssh is the most common.)

Viewing Processes

ps	List process.
uptime	View the system uptime and CPU load.
w	List active processes for all users.
top	Monitor resource-intensive processes interactively.

A *process* is a unit of work in OS X. Each program you run represents one or more processes, and OS X provides commands for viewing and manipulating them. Every process is identified by a numeric *process ID*, or PID. If your Mac seems unusually slow, the commands in this section can help identify the cause.

Processes are different from jobs (see "Shell Job Control" on page 38): processes are part of the operating system, whereas jobs are higher-level constructs known only to the shell in which they're running. A running program comprises one or more processes; a job consists of one or more programs executed as a shell command.

---

ps   stdin   **stdout**   - file   -- opt   --help   --version

ps [*options*]

The ps command displays information about your running processes, and optionally the processes of other users:

```
→ ps
  PID TTY           TIME CMD
 4706 ttys000   00:00:01 bash
15007 ttys000   00:00:00 emacs
16729 ttys000   00:00:00 ps
```

ps has at least 80 options; we'll cover just a few useful combinations. To view your processes:

→ **ps -x**

all of user smith's processes:

→ **ps -u smith**

all occurrences of a program:

→ **ps -axc | grep -w *program_name***

processes on terminal ttys000:

→ **ps -ts000**

particular processes 1, 2, and 3505:

→ **ps -p1,2,3505**

and all processes and their threads:

→ **ps -axM**

uptime stdin **stdout** - file -- opt --help --version

uptime

The uptime command tells you how long the system has been running since the last boot, and displays the *load average*, a measure of how busy your processor is. If your Mac seems slow, run uptime and the load average will tell you if it's due to heavy load on the processor:

```
→ uptime
 10:54pm  up 8 days,  3:44,  3 users,  load average: 0.89,
 1.00, 2.15
```

This information is, from left to right: the current time (10:54pm), system uptime (8 days, 3 hours, 44 minutes), number of users logged in (3), and system load average for three time periods: one minute (0.89), five minutes (1.00), and fifteen minutes (2.15). The load average is the average number of processes ready to run in that time interval.

---

w stdin **stdout** - file -- opt --help --version

w [*username*]

The w command displays the current process running in each shell for all logged-in users:

```
→ w
 10:51pm  up 8 days,  3:42,  8 users,
 load averages: 0.24 0.52 0.53
 USER     TTY     FROM   LOGIN@  IDLE   WHAT
 barrett  console -      Thu22   27:13  emacs
 jones    s000    host1 6Sep03   2:33   -
 smith    s001    host2 6Sep03   -      w
```

The top line is the same one printed by uptime. The columns indicate the user's terminal, originating host (if applicable), login time, idle time, and the current process. Provide a username to see only that user's information.

Useful options

-h Don't print the header line.

---

top [*options*]

The top command lets you monitor the most active processes, updating the display at regular intervals (say, every second). If your
Mac seems slow, top will tell you which process, if any, is to blame.
It is a screen-based program that updates the display in place, interactively. top first displays general system information about CPU
and memory usage:

```
→ top
Processes: 81 total, 2 running, 1 stuck, 78 sleeping, …
2012/03/12 22:28:03
Load Avg: 0.36, 0.43, 0.48
CPU usage: 8.10% user, 21.62% sys, 70.27% idle
SharedLibs: 632K resident, 0B data, 0B linkedit.
MemRegions: 48380 total, 1582M resident, 29M private, …
PhysMem: 891M wired, 2095M active, 770M inactive, …
VM: 189G vsize, 1091M framework vsize, 21497(0) pageins, …
Networks: packets: 53842/12M in, 63096/41M out.
Disks: 4550433/439G read, 985283/54G written.
```

and follows it with a list of running processes:

```
PID    COMMAND       %CPU TIME      … RPRVT  RSHRD  RSIZE
42652  top           8.8  00:00.89 … 1392K  216K   2108K
42206  sshd          0.0  00:00.05 … 456K   1632K  3036K
41202  Address Book  0.0  00:01.41 … 13M    13M    22M
39720- Microsoft Wo  0.6  05:38.03 … 409M   55M    670M
…
```

While top is running, you can press keys to change its behavior
interactively, such as setting the update speed (s) or sorting by a
particular column (o). Type ? to see a complete list and q to quit.

Useful options

-l *N*   Perform *N* updates, then quit.

           The command top -l1 > outfile saves a quick snapshot to a file.

-s *N*   Update the display every *N* seconds.

-pid *N*   Display only the processes with PID *N*.

Controlling Processes

open	Open any file in its default Mac application.
kill	Terminate a process (or send it a signal).
nice	Invoke a program at a particular priority.
renice	Change a process's priority as it runs.
shutdown	Reboot or halt the computer.

Once processes are started, they can be paused, restarted, terminated, and reprioritized. We discussed some of these operations as handled by the shell in "Shell Job Control" on page 38. Now we cover killing and reprioritizing.

---

open

stdin   stdout   - file   -- opt   --help   --version

```
open [options] [files] [--args application_arguments]
```

The open command opens the given files with whatever application is registered to do so. For example, open myfile.txt runs TextEdit, open spreadsheet.xls launches Microsoft Excel or Apple's Numbers, and open /Users/smith/Documents opens the Finder to display that folder. The application launches in the background so you get your shell prompt back.

You can also open a URL, launching your default web browser:

→ **open http://www.apple.com**

Useful options

-a *app*	Open the files with the given application *app* instead of the default one. If you omit the filename after -a, the application is simply launched.
-e	Open with TextEdit.
-f	Read from standard input into your default text editor. Useful as the last step of a shell pipeline.
-W	Open the application in the foreground for the shell. By default, it opens in the background so you get your shell prompt back.

```
kill [options] [process_ids]
```

The kill command sends a signal to a process, given its process ID (PID). This can terminate a process (the default action), interrupt it, suspend it, crash it, and so on. You must own the process, or be the superuser, to affect it. Remember our story in the introduction about terminating a hung Microsoft Word? We used a kill command (actually killall, described shortly) for this purpose, since it can succeed when other more common methods have failed.

To terminate the process with PID 13243, for example, run:

```
→ kill 13243
```

You can also terminate a shell job (see "Shell Job Control" on page 38) by its job number, preceded by a percent sign to distinguish it from a PID:

```
→ kill %2
```

If kill does not work—some programs catch this signal without terminating—add the option -KILL or (equivalently) -9:

```
→ kill -KILL 13243
```

which is virtually guaranteed to work. However, this is not a clean exit for the program, which may leave system resources allocated (or cause other inconsistencies) upon its death.

If you don't know the PID of a process, run ps and examine the output:

```
→ ps -ax | grep emacs
```

or even better, try the killall command, which looks up all processes for a given program by its name and kills them:

```
→ killall less
[1]+  Terminated: 15          less -c myfile
```

In addition to the kill program in the filesystem (usually /bin/kill), most shells have built-in kill commands, but their syntax and behavior differ. However, they all support the following usage:

```
→ kill -N PID
→ kill -NAME PID
```

where *N* is a signal number, and *NAME* is a signal name without its leading "SIG" (e.g., use -HUP to send the SIGHUP signal). To see a complete list of signals transmitted by kill, run kill -1, though its output differs depending on which kill you're running. For descriptions of some signals, run man kill.

---

nice

stdin   **stdout**   - file   -- opt   --help   --version

nice [-n *level*] *command_line*

When invoking a system-intensive program, you can be nice to the other processes (and users) by lowering its priority. That's what the nice command is for: it sets a *nice level* (an amount of "niceness") for a process so it gets less attention from the OS X process scheduler.[15] Here's an example of setting a big job to run at nice level 7:

→ **nice -n 7 sort VeryLargeFile > outfile**

If you run nice without a level, 10 is used. Normal processes (run without nice) run at level zero. The superuser can also lower the nice level, increasing a process's priority:

→ **sudo nice -n -10 myprogram**

To see the nice levels of your jobs, use ps and look at the "NI" column:

→ **ps -o pid,user,args,nice**

---

renice

stdin   **stdout**   - file   -- opt   --help   --version

renice [+-*N*] [*options*] *PID*

While the nice command can invoke a program at a given nice level, renice changes the nice level of an already-running process. Here we increase the nice level (decrease the priority) of process 28734 by five:

→ **renice +5 -p 28734**

---

15. This is called "nicing" the process. You'll hear the term used as a verb: "That process was niced to 12."

Ordinary users can increase the nice level of their own processes, while the superuser can also decrease it (increasing the priority) and can operate on any process. The valid range is –20 to +20, but avoid high negative numbers or you might interfere with vital system processes.

Useful options

-p *pid*   Affect the given process ID. You can omit the -p and just provide a PID (`renice +5 28734`).

-u *username*   Affect all processes owned by the given user.

---

shutdown   stdin **stdout** -file --opt --help --version

shutdown [*options*] *time* [*message*]

The shutdown command shuts down or reboots OS X; only the superuser may run it. Here's a command to shut down the system in 10 minutes, broadcasting the message "scheduled maintenance" to all users logged in:

→ `sudo shutdown -h +10 "scheduled maintenance"`

The *time* may be a number of minutes preceded by a plus sign, like +10; an absolute time in hours and minutes, like 16:25; or the word now to mean immediately.

With no options, just a time, shutdown puts the system into single-user mode, a special maintenance mode in which only one person is logged in (on the desktop), and all nonessential services are off.

→ `sudo shutdown now`

To exit single-user mode, either perform another shutdown to halt or reboot, or type ^D to bring up the system in normal, multiuser mode.

Useful options

-r   Reboot the system.

-h   Halt the system.

Scheduling Jobs

sleep	Wait a set number of seconds, doing nothing.
at	Schedule a job for a single, future time.
crontab	Schedule jobs for many future times.
launchctl	Control system services.

If you need to launch programs at particular times or at regular intervals, OS X provides several scheduling tools on the command line with various degrees of complexity.

---

sleep
stdin   stdout   - file   -- opt   **--help**   **--version**

sleep *seconds*

The sleep command simply waits a set number of seconds:

> → **sleep 5**   *Do nothing for 5 seconds*

sleep is useful for delaying a command for a set amount of time, say if you want to run something after you've stepped away from the keyboard:

> → **sleep 10 && echo 'Ten seconds have passed.'**
> *(10 seconds pass)*
> Ten seconds have passed.

---

at
stdin   **stdout**   - file   -- opt   --help   --version

at [*options*] *time_specification*

The at command runs a list of shell commands once at a specified time. It reads its shell commands from standard input, so press ^D when you're finished typing them:

> → **at 7am**
> **echo Remember to go shopping | mail smith**
> **lpr $HOME/shopping-list**
> ^D
> job 559 at 2012-07-14 21:30

Of course, you can send commands to at using a pipeline:

```
→ echo lpr myfile | at 7am
```

The commands run *in the background*, not in your current shell, so they are not interactive. You cannot see anything they print (say, using echo) unless you redirect the output to a file or pipe it to another program that can communicate with you (such as mail in our example). Likewise, you cannot provide input to these commands from the keyboard.

The time specifications understood by at are enormously flexible. In general, you can specify:

- A time followed by a date (not a date followed by a time)
- Only a date (assumes the current clock time)
- Only a time (assumes the very next occurrence, whether today or tomorrow)
- A special word like now, midnight, or teatime (16:00)
- Any of the preceding followed by an offset, like "+ 3 days"

Dates are acceptable in many forms: december 25 2012, december 25, 12/25/2012, 25.12.2012, today, thursday, and more. Month names can be abbreviated to three letters (jan, feb, mar, ...). Times are also flexible: 8pm, 8 pm, 8:00pm, 8:00 pm, 20:00, and 2000 are equivalent. Offsets are a plus or minus sign followed by whitespace and an amount of time, such as + 2 weeks.

If you don't specify a part of the date or time, at copies the missing information from the system date and time. So thursday means the upcoming Thursday at the current clock time, december 25 means the next upcoming December 25, and 4:30pm means the very next occurrence of 4:30 p.m. in the future.

The command you supply to at is not evaluated by the shell until execution time, so wildcards, variables, and other shell constructs are not expanded until then. Also, your current environment (see printenv) is preserved within each job so it executes as if you were logged in. Aliases, however, aren't available to at jobs, so don't include them.

To list your at jobs, use atq ("at queue"):

```
→ atq
559  Tue Mar 13 20:54:00 2012
```

To display the shell commands associated with an at job, use the
-c option:

```
→ at -c 559
echo Remember to go shopping | mail smith
lpr $HOME/shopping-list
```

To delete an at job, run atrm ("at remove") with the job number:

```
→ atrm 559
```

Useful options

-f *filename*	Read commands from the given file instead of standard input.
-c *job_number*	Print the job commands to standard output.

---

crontab stdin **stdout** **- file** **-- opt** --help --version

crontab [*options*] [*file*]

The crontab command, like at, schedules jobs for specific times.
However, crontab is for recurring jobs, such as "Run this command
at midnight on the second Tuesday of each month." To make this
work, you edit and save a file (called your *crontab file*), which automatically gets installed in a system directory (*/var/at/tabs*). Once
a minute, an OS X process called cron wakes up, checks your crontab file, and executes any jobs that are due:

→ **crontab -e**
    Edit your crontab file in your default editor ($EDITOR)

→ **crontab -l**
    Print your crontab file on standard output

→ **crontab -r**
    Delete your crontab file

→ **crontab myfile**
    Install the file *myfile* as your crontab file

→ **`sudo crontab`** ...
> Work with the root user's crontab file to run administrative system processes

→ **`sudo crontab -u smith`** ...
> Work with user smith's crontab file

Crontab files contain one job per line. (Blank lines and comment lines beginning with "#" are ignored.) Each line has six fields, separated by whitespace. The first five fields specify the time to run the job, and the last is the job command itself. The first five fields are:

Minutes of the hour
> Integers between 0 and 59. This can be a single number (`30`), a sequence of numbers separated by commas (`0,15,30,45`), a range (`20-30`), a sequence of ranges (`0-15,50-59`), or an asterisk to mean "all." You can also specify "every *n*th time" with the suffix `/n`; for instance, both `*/12` and `0-59/12` mean `0,12,24,36,48` (i.e., every 12 minutes).

Hours of the day
> Same syntax as for minutes.

Days of the month
> Integers between 1 and 31; again, you may use sequences, ranges, sequences of ranges, or an asterisk.

Months of the year
> Integers between 1 and 12; again, you may use sequences, ranges, sequences of ranges, or an asterisk. Additionally, you may use three-letter abbreviations (`jan`, `feb`, `mar`, ...), but not in ranges or sequences.

Days of the week
> Integers between 0 (Sunday) and 6 (Saturday); again, you may use sequences, ranges, sequences of ranges, or an asterisk. Additionally, you may use three-letter abbreviations (`sun`, `mon`, `tue`, ...), but not in ranges or sequences.

Command to execute
> Any shell command, which will be executed in your login environment, so you can refer to environment variables like `$HOME` and expect them to work. Use only absolute paths to

your commands (e.g., */usr/bin/who* instead of who) as a general rule.

Here is a line from a crontab file that runs a backup with rsync every Sunday at 1:30 a.m. We provide the absolute path to the rsync program to ensure that the cron program finds it, a good practice with all crontab entries.

```
30   1   *   *   sun   /usr/bin/rsync -a -E / server:
```

Here are more example time specifications. Each would be followed by a command to execute:

*	*	*	*	*	Every minute
45	*	*	*	*	45 minutes after each hour (1:45, 2:45, etc.)
45	9	*	*	*	Every day at 9:45 a.m.
45	9	8	*	*	The eighth day of every month at 9:45 a.m.
45	9	8	12	*	Every December 8 at 9:45 a.m.
45	9	8	dec	*	Every December 8 at 9:45 a.m.
45	9	*	*	6	Every Saturday at 9:45 a.m.
45	9	*	*	sat	Every Saturday at 9:45 a.m.
45	9	*	12	6	Every Saturday in December, at 9:45 a.m.
45	9	8	12	6	Every Saturday in December, plus December 8, at 9:45 a.m.

If the command produces any output upon execution, cron will email it to the user who owns the *crontab* file.

---

launchctl
stdin   stdout   - file   -- opt   --help   --version

```
launchctl [subcommand [arguments]]
```

The launchctl command (pronounced "launch control") sets up programs to run automatically according to a schedule or other rules. It is similar to cron but more flexible and complex. It's also made for the Mac whereas cron comes from a Unix/Linux background. Its full operation is beyond the scope of this book, but we'll show you the basics.

Launching a program requires several parts:

- A program to be launched.
- A property list or *plist* file that specifies how the program gets launched, written in XML.
- Specifying whether to run as an *agent* or a *daemon*. An agent is associated with a particular user and can have a graphical user interface (GUI). A daemon is not associated with a user and cannot have a GUI.
- The system service `launchd`, which controls all the launched programs.
- The `launchctl` command, a front-end to `launchd`, which handles *plist* files.

plist files are found in several system directories, including */Library/LaunchAgents*, */Library/LaunchDaemons*, */System/Library/LaunchAgents*, and */System/Library/LaunchDaemons*. If you write or install personal *plist* files, they go into *$HOME/Library/LaunchAgents* or *$HOME/Library/LaunchDaemons*. An example *plist* file is */System/Library/LaunchDaemons/ssh.plist*, which turns the SSH server on and off. In "Enabling remote logins" on page 184, we enable the SSH server via System Preferences, but you could also start it with the command:

```
→ sudo launchctl load \
  /System/Library/LaunchDaemons/ssh.plist
```

and terminate it with:

```
→ sudo launchctl unload \
  /System/Library/LaunchDaemons/ssh.plist
```

What do *plist* files look like? Here is an example for a trivial task: running the `date` program every 10 seconds, writing the output to a file */tmp/date.log*:

```
<?xml version="1.0" encoding="UTF-8"?>            Required
<!DOCTYPE plist PUBLIC                            Required
 -//Apple Computer//DTD PLIST 1.0//EN             Required
 http://www.apple.com/DTDs/PropertyList-1.0.dtd"> Required
<plist version="1.0">                             Required
<dict>                                            Begin properties
    <key>label</key>                              Name of job
    <string>com.example.date</string>
```

```
    <key>ProgramArguments</key>                    Program to run
    <array>
        <string>/bin/date</string>
    </array>

    <key>Nice</key>                                 Niceness level
    <integer>1</integer>                            (see "nice" on page 12

    <key>StartInterval</key>                        How often to run
    <integer>10</integer>                           (in seconds)

    <key>StandardOutPath</key>                      File for stdout
    <string>/tmp/date.log</string>
</dict>                                             End of properties
</plist>
```

Let's name the preceding *plist* file *com.example.date.plist* and store it in the directory *$HOME/Library/LaunchAgents*. To make sure the *plist* file has correct syntax, run the plutil command:

```
→ plutil -lint com.example.date.plist
com.example.date.plist: OK
```

Then launch the process with launchctl:

```
→ cd $HOME/Library/LaunchAgents
→ launchctl load com.example.date.plist
```

If you watch the output file specified in the *plist* file, */tmp/date.log*, you'll see that it receives a date every 10 seconds or so:

```
→ tail -f /tmp/date.log
Tue Mar 20 20:41:14 EDT 2012
Tue Mar 20 20:41:25 EDT 2012
Tue Mar 20 20:41:36 EDT 2012
```

Exciting, isn't it? When you want this to stop, run:

```
→ launchctl unload com.example.date.plist
```

To perform launchctl commands automatically when the Macintosh boots, put them into *$HOME/.launchd.conf* (for yourself) or */etc/launchd.conf* (for system processes), one per line.

This was a simplified example. *plist* files have 50 types of keys, and launchctl supports over 20 subcommands. See the manpage for more details, and for the full syntax of *plist* files, run man launchd.plist.

Useful subcommands

load *F*	Tell launchd to load the *plist* file *F*.
unload *F*	Tell launchd to unload the *plist* file *F*.
list	List all jobs currently loaded in launchd

Users and Their Environment

logname	Print your login name.
whoami	Print your current, effective username.
id	Print the user ID and group membership of a user.
who	List logged-in users, long output.
users	List logged-in users, short output.
last	Determine when someone last logged in.
finger	Print information about users.
chfn	Change a user's personal information.
passwd	Change a password.
chsh	Change a user's shell.
dscl	Create, modify, and delete users.
printenv	Print your environment.

How many user accounts are set up on your Macintosh? For many Mac owners, the answer is "one."[16] Nevertheless, any Macintosh can have multiple user accounts for family, co-workers, or beloved pets. OS X is a full-fledged multiuser operating system, meaning that multiple people can work a single Macintosh at the same time. While one person is using the connected display, keyboard, and mouse (known as the *console*), others can log in remotely and run shells and commands (discussed in "Running a Shell Remotely" on page 183). Each user is identified by a unique *username*, like "smith" or

---

16. Not counting the Guest User, which is installed with OS X.

"funkyguy," and owns a (reasonably) private part of the system for doing work (*/Users/smith*, */Users/funkyguy*, etc.).

This section's grab-bag of programs tells you all about *users*: their names, login times, and properties of their environment. Several other commands let you change a user's password, default shell, and personal details.

---

logname
stdin **stdout** - file -- opt --help --version

```
logname
```

The logname command prints your login name:

```
→ logname
smith
```

---

whoami
stdin **stdout** - file -- opt --help --version

```
whoami
```

The whoami command prints the name of the current, effective user. This may differ from your login name (the output of logname) if you've used the sudo command. The following example distinguishes whoami from logname. In normal situations, they both print your username:

```
→ logname
smith
→ whoami
smith
```

When you become the root user via sudo, then effectively you are the root user, and whoami indicates this:

```
→ sudo logname
smith
→ sudo whoami
root
```

id [*options*] [*username*]

Every user has a unique, numeric *user ID*, and a default group with a unique, numeric *group ID*. The id command prints these values along with their associated user and group names:

```
→ id
uid=500(smith) gid=20(staff)
groups=20(staff),402(com.apple.sharepoint.group.1),…

→ sudo id
uid=0(root) gid=0(wheel)
groups=0(wheel),402(com.apple.sharepoint.group.1),…
```

Useful options

- -u   Print the effective user ID and exit.

- -g   Print the effective group ID and exit.

- -G   Print the IDs of all other groups to which the user belongs.

- -n   Print names (for users and groups) rather than numeric IDs. Must be combined with -u, -g, or -G. For example, id -Gn produces the same output as the groups command.

- -r   Print login values instead of effective values. Must be combined with -u, -g, or -G.

---

who [*options*] [*filename*]

The who command lists all logged-in users, one line per login shell:

```
→ who
smith    console   Sep  6 17:09
barrett  ttys000   Sep  6 17:10 (example.com)
jones    ttys001   Sep  8 20:58 (192.168.13.7)
jones    ttys002   Sep  3 05:11 (192.168.13.7)
```

Normally, who gets its data from the file */var/run/utmpx*. The *filename* argument can specify a different data file, if you happen to have one in the right format.

Useful options

-H   Print a row of headings as the first line.

-u   Also print each user's idle time at his/her terminal.

-T   Also indicate whether each user's terminal is writable (see mesg in "Messaging" on page 168). A plus sign means yes, a minus sign means no, and a question mark means unknown.

-m   Display information only about yourself, i.e., the user associated with the current terminal.

-q   Quick display of usernames only, and a count of users. Much like the users command, but it adds a count.

---

users   stdin   **stdout**   - file   -- opt   --help   --version

users

The users command prints a quick listing of users who have login sessions:

```
→ users
barrett jones smith
```

Like the who command, users reads the file */var/run/utmpx*.

---

last   stdin   **stdout**   - file   **-- opt**   --help   --version

last [options] [users]

The last command displays a history of logins, in reverse chronological order.

```
→ last
dan   ttys003  example.com  Mon Sep 8 21:07 - 21:08 (00:01)
lisa  console               Mon Sep 8 20:25 - 20:56 (00:31)
dan   ttys001  example.com  Sun Sep 7 22:19 still logged in
...
```

You may provide usernames or tty names to limit the output.

Useful options

-N   Print only the latest N lines of output, where N is a positive integer.

-t *tty*   Print entries only for the given tty name, such as ttys001.

---

finger

finger [*options*] [*user*[@*host*]]

The finger command prints information about logged-in users in
a short form:

```
→ finger
Login      Name            TTY    Idle  Login   Time    Phone
smith      Sandy Smith     *con         Sep 6   17:09
barrett    Daniel Barrett  s00    24    Sep 6   17:10
jones      Jill Jones      s01          Thu     20:58
```

or a long form:

```
→ finger smith
Login: smith                         Name: Sandy Smith
Directory: /Users/smith              Shell: /bin/bash
On since Sat Sep  6 17:09 (EDT) on console
No Mail.
Project: Enhance world peace
Plan: Mistrust first impulses; they are always right.
```

The *user* argument can be a local username or a remote user in the
form *user@host*. However, most computers no longer allow finger
connections from the outside world due to security concerns.

Useful options

-l   Print in long format.

-s   Print in short format.

-p   Don't display the Project and Plan sections, which are ordinarily read from the user's
      ~/.project and ~/.plan files, respectively.

---

chfn

chfn [*options*] [*username*]

The chfn (change finger) command updates a few pieces of personal
information maintained by the system: real name, home telephone,
office telephone, and office location, as displayed by the finger

command.[17] Invoked without a username, chfn affects your account; invoked with a username (by the superuser), it affects that user. With no options, chfn will prompt you for the desired information:

```
→ chfn
Password: ********
Name [Shawn Smith]: Shawn E. Smith
Office [100 Barton Hall]:
Office Phone [212-555-1212]: 212-555-1234
Home Phone []:
```

Useful options

-f *name*   Change the full name to *name*.

-h *phone*   Change the home phone number to *phone*.

-p *phone*   Change the office phone number to *phone*.

-o *office*   Change the office location to *office*.

---

passwd   stdin   **stdout**   - file   -- opt   --help   --version

passwd [*options*] [*username*]

The passwd command changes a login password, yours by default:

    → **passwd**

or another user's password if run by an administrator:

    → **sudo passwd smith**

---

chsh   stdin   **stdout**   - file   **-- opt**   --help   --version

chsh [*options*] [*username*]

The chsh (change shell) command sets your login shell program. Different shells have different capabilities, and if you're familiar with a different shell from another operating system (say, Linux), you might want to use that shell on the Mac.

---

17. This information is stored in the OS X user database, not in your Address Book.

Invoked without a username, chsh affects your account; invoked with a username (by an administrator), it affects that user. With no options, chsh will prompt you for the desired information:

```
→ chsh
Changing shell for smith.
Password: *******
New shell [/bin/bash]: /bin/tcsh
```

The new shell must be listed in */etc/shells*.

Useful options

-s *shell* Specify the new shell.

-l List all permissible shells.

---

dscl stdin **stdout** - file -- opt --help --version

dscl [*arguments*]

The dscl command has many uses, but for our purposes, it's for creating, modifying, and deleting users. Normally you create users with System Preferences, under Users & Groups (Lion) or Accounts (earlier versions of OS X), and frankly this is the easiest method for a single user. But if you need to do it via the shell (say, for creating multiple users in bulk), dscl is the approved technique. In this section, we'll create a user on the local Macintosh. First we need to choose:

- A username. We'll use zippy.
- A password.
- A unique positive integer for the user ID. We'll use 550.
- A default group for the user to belong to. We'll use the staff group, whose group ID is 20.

There is no single command to create a user with all necessary attributes; you must issue multiple dscl commands to get the job done. First, we'll create the user:[18]

---

18. If your version of OS X is very old and these commands fail, try a slightly different syntax. Instead of localhost, supply a root slash (/), and instead of /Local/Default, write /Local.

```
→ sudo dscl localhost -create /Local/Default/Users/zippy
```

Immediately set a password so intruders cannot log in:

```
→ sudo passwd zippy
Password: *******
```

Now specify the user ID, a positive integer that must be unique, i.e., no other users on your Macintosh have the same ID. You can discover the highest user ID in use by running:

```
→ dscl . list /users UniqueID | awk '{print $2}' \
  | sort -n | tail -1
214
```

which lists all users and their IDs, extracts the second item (the IDs), sorts them numerically, and then prints the last (highest) ID. Choose a new ID higher than 500, since users with lower IDs don't show up in System Preferences, and you might want to manage the user later. Once you've chosen an ID (say, 550), run:

```
→ sudo dscl localhost -create /Local/Default/Users/zippy \
  UniqueID 550
```

Next, specify the user's default group ID:

```
→ sudo dscl localhost -create /Local/Default/Users/zippy \
  PrimaryGroupID 20
```

Choose a shell for the user, generally bash:

```
→ sudo dscl localhost -create /Local/Default/Users/zippy \
  UserShell /bin/bash
```

Set the user's real name:

```
→ sudo dscl localhost -create /Local/Default/Users/zippy \
  RealName 'Zippy D. Doodah'
```

Finally, set and create the user's home directory:

```
→ sudo dscl localhost -create /Local/Default/Users/zippy \
  NFSHomeDirectory /Users/zippy
→ sudo mkdir /Users/zippy
→ sudo chown zippy:staff /Users/zippy
```

and you're done! Run System Preferences, look under Users & Groups (Lion) or Accounts (earlier versions of OS X), and user zippy should show up. You can also see zippy's details by running finger:

```
→ finger zippy
```

or see more technical output with `dscl`:

```
→ sudo dscl localhost -read /Local/Default/Users/zippy
```

To turn the user into an administrator, use System Preferences or run the `dseditgroup` command:

```
→ sudo dseditgroup -o edit -t user -a zippy admin
```

To delete a user, run `dscl`, then optionally delete the user's home directory:

```
→ sudo dscl localhost -delete /Local/Default/Users/zippy
→ sudo rm -rf /Users/zippy
```

The user is now gone:

```
→ finger zippy
finger: zippy: no such user
→ sudo dscl localhost -read /Local/Default/Users/zippy
<dscl_cmd> DS Error: -14136 (eDSRecordNotFound)
```

---

printenv   stdin **stdout** -file --opt --help --version

`printenv [environment_variable]`

The `printenv` command prints all environment variables known to your shell and their values:

```
→ printenv
HOME=/Users/smith
MAIL=/var/spool/mail/smith
NAME=Sandy Smith
SHELL=/bin/bash
...
```

or a specified variable:

```
→ printenv HOME
/Users/smith
```

Becoming the Superuser

Every Macintosh has a special user named *root*—the *super-user* or *administrator* on a Macintosh—who has the privileges to do anything at all on the system. Ordinary users are restricted: they can run most programs, but in general they can modify only the files they own. An administrator, on the other hand, can create, modify, or delete any file and run any program on a given Mac.

If you administer your Mac, you might never need to use the root account.[19] Rather, any account can be set up with administrator privileges (also called *root privileges*) and have all the same power as root. To do this, run System Preferences, visit Users & Groups (Lion) or Accounts (earlier versions of OS X), select the desired user, and check the checkbox "Allow user to administer this computer." (Only an administrator can elevate other users to be administrators.)

Any user who is an administrator can easily become the superuser and run arbitrary commands. You needn't log out and log back in to do this; just preface any shell command with sudo and provide your password:

```
→ sudo command here
Password: *******
```

For example:

```
→ ls /private/secrets              View a protected directory
ls: secrets: Permission denied       It failed
→ sudo ls /private/secrets         Try with sudo
Password: *******
secretfile1    secretfile2            It worked!
```

After the command has run, you'll be your ordinary self again, with one extra bonus. Future sudo commands will not prompt for your password, making it easier to run multiple sudo commands in a row. This special power lasts for five minutes after your last sudo command, after which sudo will prompt for passwords again.

If you plan to run many superuser commands and don't want to type "sudo" all the time, run a shell as root:

```
→ sudo /bin/bash
```

19. In fact, it is disabled by default.

so every command you execute runs as root. Be careful to terminate this shell (by typing ^D or **exit**) when you're finished, so nobody else can walk up and run superuser commands with it.

If you provide a username to **sudo**:

→ `sudo -u sophia command here`

you will run the command as that user, rather than as an administrator.

The behavior of **sudo** is configurable in complex ways. You can exercise precise control over privileges (in the */etc/sudoers* file) and even keep a log of the commands that get run. A full discussion is beyond the scope of this book: if you would like to read more, see `man sudo` and visit *http://www.gratisoft.us/sudo/* for full details.

Useful options

-u *username*	Run the command as the given user.
-b	Run the command in the background.

Group Management

groups	Print the group membership of a user.
dscl	Create, modify, and delete groups.

A *group* is a set of accounts treated as a single entity. If you give permission for a group to take some action (such as modify a file), then all members of that group can take it. For example, you can give full permissions for the group **friends** to read, write, and execute the file */tmp/sample*:

```
→ groups
users smith friends
→ chgrp friends /tmp/sample
→ chmod 770 /tmp/sample
```

```
→ ls -l /tmp/sample
-rwxrwx--- 1 smith friends  2874 Oct 20 22:35 /tmp/sample
```

To add users to a group, use **dscl**. To change the group ownership of a file, recall the **chgrp** commands from "File Properties" on page 68.

---

groups
stdin **stdout** - file -- opt --help --version

```
groups [usernames]
```

The groups command prints the OS X groups to which you belong, or to which other users belong:

```
→ whoami
smith
→ groups
smith users
→ groups jones root
jones : jones users
root : root bin daemon sys adm disk wheel src
```

---

dscl
stdin **stdout** - file -- opt --help --version

```
dscl [arguments]
```

We encountered the dscl command in "Users and Their Environment" on page 137 when creating and deleting users. It can also create and delete groups. As with users, you must run multiple commands to make a group. Suppose we want a new group named gang. First do the initial creation:

```
→ sudo dscl localhost -create /Local/Default/Groups/gang
```

Give the group the password *, meaning a non-functional password, and a unique positive integer ID:

```
→ sudo dscl localhost -create /Local/Default/Groups/gang \
  passwd '*'
→ sudo dscl localhost -create /Local/Default/Groups/gang \
  gid 301
```

Now add the local user zippy to the group, and check the result with the groups command:

```
→ sudo dscl localhost -create /Local/Default/Groups/gang \
  GroupMembership zippy
```

Now confirm that zippy is a member of the group:

```
→ groups zippy
... gang ...
```

To delete the group, run:

```
→ sudo dscl localhost -delete /Local/Default/Groups/gang
```

You can also list all groups:

```
→ dscl . list /groups
```

Host Information

uname	Print basic system information.
sw_vers	Print the Macintosh software version.
hostname	Print the system's hostname.
scutil	Set or get host information.
ifconfig	Set and display network interface information.
ipconfig	Set and display network interface information for debugging.

Every Macintosh (or *host*) has a name, a network IP address, and other properties. Here's how to display this information.

---

uname   stdin   **stdout**   -file   --opt   --help   --version

```
uname [options]
```

The uname command prints fundamental information about the lowest level of the OS X operating system, known as the *kernel*:

```
→ uname -a
Darwin mymac.home 11.3.0 Darwin Kernel Version 11.3.0:
  Thu Jan 12 18:47:41 PST 2012; root:xnu-1699.24.23~1
  /RELEASE_X86_64 x86_64
```

This includes the kernel name (Darwin), hostname (mymac.home), kernel release (11.3.0), and kernel version (Darwin Kernel Version

---

11.3.0: Thu Jan 12 ...). Each of these values can be printed individually using options.

Useful options

-a   All information.

-s   Only the kernel name (the default).

-n   Only the hostname, as with the hostname command.

-r   Only the kernel release number.

-v   Only the kernel version.

-m   Only the hardware name, e.g., x86_64.

-p   Only the processor type, e.g., i386.

---

sw_vers
stdin   stdout   - file   -- opt   --help   --version

sw_vers [*options*]

The sw_vers command displays the OS X software version on your Macintosh:

```
→ sw_vers
ProductName:    Mac OS X
ProductVersion: 10.7.3
BuildVersion:   11D50
```

Useful options

-productName   Print only the product name.

-productVersion   Print only the product version.

-buildVersion   Print only the build version.

---

hostname
stdin   **stdout**   - file -- opt   --help   --version

hostname [*options*] [*name*]

The hostname command prints the network name of your computer:

```
→ hostname
myhost.example.com
```

---

or your short hostname, which is the computer name you set in System Preferences (under Sharing):

```
→ hostname -s
myhost
```

You can also set your hostname, as root:

```
→ sudo hostname orange
```

This change is temporary and will not survive a reboot. To make it permanent, run the scutil command or use System Preferences (under Sharing).

Hostnames and nameservers are complicated topics well beyond the scope of this book. Don't just blindly start setting hostnames!

Useful options

-s Print your host's short name.

---

scutil   stdin   stdout   -file   --opt   --help   --version

scutil [*options*] [*arguments*]

The scutil command ("system configuration utility") can display basic network information, set the computer hostname, and perform several other tasks. For example, view your computer name with:

```
→ scutil --get ComputerName
My Macintosh
```

change the computer name with:

```
→ sudo scutil --set ComputerName banana
```

check if another host is reachable from your Mac (though the ping command is more informative):

```
→ scutil -r www.apple.com
Reachable
```

or view technical DNS information with:

```
→ scutil --dns
DNS configuration
resolver #1
  search domain[0] : home
```

```
    nameserver[0] : 192.168.1.1
resolver #2
...
```

The program has other uses as well, like interacting with the system
configuration daemon (configd), but they are beyond the scope of
this book.

---

ifconfig   stdin   **stdout**   - file   -- opt   --help   --version

```
ifconfig [options] interface
```

The ifconfig displays information about your network interfaces,
such as IP addresses. We'll cover a few simple commands here, but
networking in general is beyond the scope of this book.

To display information about the default network interface (usually
called en0 or en1):

```
→ ifconfig en0
en0: flags=8823<UP,BROADCAST,SMART,RUNNING,SIMPLEX>
    options=4<VLAN_MTU>
    ether 00:25:4b:fd:44:6c
    inet6 fe80::225:4bff:fefd:446c%en1 prefixlen 64
    inet 192.168.1.7 netmask 0xffffff00
    media: autoselect (100baseTX <full-duplex,flow-control>)
    status: active
```

This includes your MAC address (00:25:4b:fd:44:6c), your IP address (192.168.1.7), your netmask (0xffffff00, which is hexadecimal
for 255.255.255.0), and various other information. To view all
loaded network interfaces, run:

```
→ ifconfig -a
```

---

ipconfig   stdin   **stdout**   - file   -- opt   --help   --version

```
ipconfig action [arguments]
```

The ipconfig command displays and sets various aspects of your
computer's network interface. This command is *only for testing and
debugging*, and the whole topic is beyond the scope of this book,
but we'll teach you a few tricks. To see the IP address and subnet
mask of the network interface en0, try:

```
→ ipconfig getifaddr en0
192.168.1.7
→ ipconfig getoption en0 subnet_mask
255.255.255.0
```

or to count your network interfaces, run:

```
→ ipconfig ifcount
2
```

To display the IP address of your Mac's primary DNS server, and your Mac's domain name, run:

```
→ ipconfig getoption en0 domain_name_server
192.168.1.1
→ ipconfig getoption en0 domain_name
example.com
```

To view the DHCP information that your Mac received from a DHCP server, run:

```
→ ipconfig getpacket en0
op = BOOTREPLY
htype = 1
flags = 0
hlen = 6
...
```

Most other `ipconfig` actions, such as changing parameters of your network interface, require more technical knowledge of networking.

Host Location

host	Look up hostnames, IP addresses, and DNS info.
whois	Look up the registrants of Internet domains.
ping	Check if a remote host is reachable.
traceroute	View the network path to a remote host.

When dealing with remote computers, you might want to know more about them. Who owns them? What are the IP addresses? Where on the network are they located?

host [*options*] *name* [*server*]

The host command looks up the hostname or IP address of a remote machine by querying DNS:

```
→ host apple.com
apple.com has address 17.172.224.47
apple.com has address 17.149.160.49
→ host 17.172.224.47
47.224.172.17.in-addr.arpa domain name pointer apple.com.
```

It can also find out much more:

```
→ host -a apple.com
Trying "apple.com"
;; ->>HEADER<<- opcode: QUERY, status: NOERROR, id: 2915
;; flags: qr rd ra; QUERY: 1, ANSWER: 2, …

;; QUESTION SECTION:
;apple.com.                        IN      ANY

;; ANSWER SECTION:
apple.com.      2003    IN      A       17.172.224.47
apple.com.      2003    IN      A       17.149.160.49

Received 59 bytes from 192.168.1.1#53 in 20 ms
```

though a full discussion of this output is beyond the scope of this book. The final, optional "server" parameter specifies a particular nameserver for the query:

```
→ host apple.com nserver.apple.com
Using domain server:
Name: nserver.apple.com
Address: 17.254.0.50#53
apple.com has address 17.149.160.49
…
```

To see all options, type host by itself.

Useful options

-a Display all available information.

-t Choose the type of nameserver query: A, AXFR, CNAME, HINFO, KEY, MX, NS, PTR, SIG, SOA, and so on.

Here's an example of the -t option to locate MX records:

```
→ host -t MX apple.com
apple.com mail is handled by 10 mail-in11.apple.com.
```

If the host command doesn't do what you want, try dig, another powerful DNS lookup utility. There's also the nslookup command, mostly obsolete but still available in OS X.

---

whois
stdin **stdout** file **--opt** --help --version

whois [*options*] *domain_name*

The whois command looks up the registration of an Internet domain:

```
→ whois itunes.com
Domain Name: ITUNES.COM
Name Server: NSERVER.APPLE.COM
Updated Date: 27-apr-2010
Creation Date: 11-aug-1998
Expiration Date: 10-aug-2019
...
```

plus a few screens full of legal disclaimers from the registrar.

Useful options

-h *registrar*	Perform the lookup at the given registrar's server. For example, whois -h whois.networksolutions.com yahoo.com.
-p *port*	Query the given the TCP port instead of the default, 43 (the whois service).

---

ping
stdin **stdout** file **--opt** --help --version

ping [*options*] *host*

The ping command tells you if a remote host is reachable. It sends small packets (ICMP packets to be precise) to a remote host and waits for responses.

```
→ ping google.com
PING google.com (74.125.226.144) from 192.168.0.10 :
56(84) bytes of data.
```

```
64 bytes from www.google.com (74.125.226.144): icmp_seq=0
  ttl=49 time=32.390 msec
64 bytes from www.google.com (74.125.226.144): icmp_seq=1
  ttl=49 time=24.208 msec
^C
--- google.com ping statistics ---
2 packets transmitted, 2 packets received, 0% packet loss
round-trip min/avg/max/mdev = 24.208/28.299/32.390/4.091 ms
```

Useful options

-c N   Ping at most N times.

-i N   Wait N seconds (default 1) between pings.

-n   Print IP addresses in the output, rather than hostnames.

---

traceroute stdin **stdout** -file **-- opt** **--help** **--version**

```
traceroute [options] host [packet_length]
```

The traceroute command prints the network path from your local
host to a remote host, and the time it takes for packets to traverse
the path.

```
→ traceroute yahoo.com
 1 server.example.com (192.168.0.20) 1.397 ms ...
 2 10.221.16.1 (10.221.16.1) 15.397 ms ...
 3 gbr2-p10.cb1ma.ip.att.net (12.123.40.190) 4.952 ms ...
...
16 p6.www.dcn.yahoo.com (216.109.118.69)  * ...
```

Each host in the path is sent three "probes" and the return times
are reported. If five seconds pass with no response, traceroute
prints an asterisk. Also, traceroute may be blocked by firewalls or
unable to proceed for various reasons, in which case it prints a
symbol:

Symbol	Meaning
!F	Fragmentation needed.
!H	Host unreachable.
!N	Network unreachable.
!P	Protocol unreachable.

Symbol	Meaning
!S	Source route failed.
!X	Communication administratively prohibited.
!N	ICMP unreachable code N.

The default packet size is 40 bytes, but you can change this with the final, optional *packet_length* parameter (e.g., `traceroute myhost 120`).

Useful options

-n	Numeric mode: print IP addresses instead of hostnames.
-w N	Change the timeout from five seconds to N seconds.

Network Connections

ssh	Securely log into a remote host, or run commands on it.
telnet	Log into a remote host (not secure!).
scp	Securely copy files to/from a remote host (batch).
sftp	Securely copy files to/from a remote host (interactive).
ftp	Copy files to/from a remote host (interactive, not secure!).

It's easy to establish network connections from one machine to another for remote logins and file transfers. Just make sure you do it securely with the commands we cover.

---

ssh   **stdin**   **stdout**   -file   --opt   --help   --version

`ssh [options] host [command]`

The ssh (Secure Shell) program securely logs you into a remote machine where you already have an account:

→ `ssh remote.example.com`

Alternatively, it can run a single command on that remote machine without needing an interactive shell. Here we rename a file:

→ `ssh remote.example.com mv file1 file2`

`ssh` encrypts all data that travels across its connection, including your username and password (which you'll need to access the remote machine). The SSH protocol also supports other ways to authenticate, such as public keys and host IDs. See `man sshd` for details.

Useful options

`-l user`	Specify your remote username; otherwise, `ssh` assumes your local username. You can also use the syntax *username@host*:

     → `ssh smith@server.example.com`

`-p port`	Use a *port* number other than the default (22).
`-t`	Allocate a tty on the remote system; useful when trying to run a remote command with an interactive user interface, such as a text editor.
`-v`	Produce verbose output, useful for debugging.

---

telnet   stdin **stdout** - file -- opt --help --version

`telnet [options] host [port]`

The `telnet` program logs you into a remote machine where you already have an account.

→ `telnet remote.example.com`

Avoid `telnet` for remote logins: most implementations are not secure and send your password over the network in plain text for anyone to steal. Use `ssh` instead, which protects your password and data via encryption. There are two exceptions:

- In a Kerberos environment, using secure ("kerberized") telnet software on both the client and server side. See *http://web.mit .edu/kerberos/* for more information.

- Connecting to a remote port when you aren't sending any sensitive information at all. For example, to check for the presence of a web server (port 80) on a remote system:

    → `telnet remote.example.com 80`
    `Trying 192.168.55.21...`
    `Connected to remote.example.com`
    `Escape character is '^]'.`

```
xxx                    Type some junk and press Enter
<HTML><HEAD>           Yep, it's a web server
<TITLE>400 Bad Request</TITLE>
</HEAD><BODY>
<H1>Bad Request</H1>
Your browser sent a request that
this server could not understand.<P>
</BODY></HTML>
Connection closed by foreign host.
```

Note that you are simply connecting to the port, not necessarily using it in a correct or meaningful way.

To discourage you further from using telnet non-securely, we aren't even going to describe its options.

---

scp

```
scp local_spec remote_spec
```

The scp (secure copy) command copies files and directories from one computer to another in batch. (For an interactive user interface, see sftp.) It encrypts all communication between the two machines using SSH, and prompts for your password as needed. As a simple example, scp can copy a local file to a remote machine (by default into your remote home directory):

→ **scp myfile remote.example.com:newfile**

recursively copy a directory to a remote machine:

→ **scp -r mydir remote.example.com:**

copy a remote file to your local machine:

→ **scp remote.example.com:myfile .**

or recursively copy a remote directory to your local machine:

→ **scp -r remote.example.com:mydir .**

If your remote username differs from your local one, use the *username@host* syntax:

→ **scp myfile smith@remote.example.com:**

Useful options

-p   Duplicate all file attributes (permissions, timestamps) when copying.

-r   Recursively copy a directory and its contents.

-v   Produce verbose output, useful for debugging.

---

sftp   **stdin**   **stdout**   -file   **--opt**   --help   --version

```
sftp (host | username@host)
```

The sftp program copies files interactively and securely between two computers. (As opposed to scp, which copies files in batch.) The user interface is much like that of ftp, but ftp is not secure.

```
→ sftp remote.example.com
Password: ********
Connected to remote.example.com.
sftp> cd MyFiles
sftp> ls
README
file1
file2
file3
sftp> get file2
Fetching /Users/smith/MyFiles/file2 to file2
sftp> quit
```

If your username on the remote system is different from your local one, use the *username@host* argument:

```
→ sftp smith@remote.example.com
```

Command	Meaning
help	View a list of available commands.
ls	List the files in the current remote directory.
lls	List the files in the current local directory.
pwd	Print the remote working directory.
lpwd	Print the local working directory.
cd *dir*	Change your remote directory to be *dir*.
lcd *dir*	Change your local directory to be *dir*.

Command	Meaning
get *file1* [*file2*]	Copy remote *file1* to local machine, optionally renamed as *file2*.
put *file1* [*file2*]	Copy local *file1* to remote machine, optionally renamed as *file2*.
mget *file**	Copy multiple remote files to the local machine using wildcards * and ?.
mput *file**	Copy multiple local files to the remote machine using wildcards * and ?.
quit	Exit sftp.

---

ftp   stdin   stdout   -file   --opt   --help   --version

ftp [*options*] *host*

The ftp (File Transfer Protocol) program copies files between computers, but not in a secure manner: your username and password travel over the network as plain text. Use sftp instead if your remote server supports it.

The same commands we listed for sftp also work for ftp. (However, the two programs support other, differing commands, too.)

Email Commands

mail   Minimal text-based mail client and command-line mailer.

mailq   View the outgoing mail queue on your system.

If you read email on your Mac, you're probably using a graphical mail application, such as Mail, or a web-based mail reader. In the Terminal, you can also run some simple, entirely text-based programs for handling email.

Before you can use these programs, your Mac's mail server software, known as postfix, will need to be configured. This is an advanced task: mail server setup is too complex for this book. If you want to attempt it, the necessary files are located in */etc/postfix*. This configuration can vary greatly depending on your mail provider and your network setup. Search the web for "postfix" and the name of your mail provider to locate setup instructions.

---

mail

mail [*options*] *recipient*

The mail program is a quick, simple email client. Most people want a more powerful program for regular use, but for quick messages from the command line or in scripts, mail is really handy.

To send a quick message:

```
→ mail smith@example.com
Subject: my subject
I'm typing a message.
To end it, I type a period by itself on a line.

.              Ends the message
EOT
→
```

To send a quick message using a single command, use a pipeline:

```
→ echo "Hello world" | mail -s "subject" smith@example.com
```

To mail a file using a single command, you can use redirection or a pipeline:

```
→ mail -s "my subject" smith@example.com < filename
→ cat filename | mail -s "my subject" smith@example.com
```

Notice how easily you can send the output of a pipeline as an email message; this is useful in scripts.

Useful options

-s *subject*	Set the subject line of an outgoing message.
-v	Verbose mode: print messages about mail delivery.
-c *addresses*	CC the message to the given addresses, a comma-separated list.
-b *addresses*	BCC the message to the given addresses, a comma-separated list.

---

mailq

```
mailq
```

The `mailq` command lists any outgoing email messages awaiting delivery:

```
→ mailq
Queue ID- --Size-- ----Arrival Time-- -Sender/Recipient--
46AAB43972*    333 Tue Jan 10 21:17:14 smith@example.com
                                        jones@elsewhere.org
```

Sent mail messages are also recorded in a log file, */var/log/mail.log*.

Beyond Mail Readers

Various commands can make email more "transparent" than on other systems that merely display your mailbox and send and receive messages. The ability to list outgoing email messages with `mailq` is just one example. Here are some other options to whet your appetite and encourage you to explore:

- You can process your mailboxes with any command-line tools, such as `grep`, because mail files are plain text.

- You can manually retrieve messages from your mail server at the command line with the `fetchmail` command. Using a simple configuration file, this command can reach out to IMAP and POP servers and download mail in batch. See `man fetchmail`.

- Your system can run a mail server, such as `postfix` or `send mail`, to handle the most complex mail delivery situations.

- You can control local mail delivery in sophisticated ways with the `procmail` command, which filters arriving email messages through any arbitrary program. See `man procmail`.

- Spam filtering can be sophisticated on OS X: check out the SpamAssassin suite of programs. You can run it personally on your incoming email, or at the server level for large numbers of users. SpamAssassin is not included in OS X but is available from *http://spamassassin.apache.org*.

In short, email is not limited to the features of your mail-reading program. Investigate and experiment!

Web Commands

curl   Download web pages and files.

wget   Download multiple web pages and files.

Your Mac comes with a web browser, Safari, and you can also install Firefox, Google Chrome, or other third party browsers. Through the Terminal, however, you can interact with the web in other ways. The two commands we cover, **curl** and **wget**, can both hit web pages and download files from the command line, but they have different features and advantages.

As a reminder, you can open any URL from the command line, launching your default web browser, with the **open** command, as we saw in "Controlling Processes" on page 126:

→ **open** http://...   *Any URL*

---

curl	stdin	stdout	- file	-- opt	--help	--version

curl [*options*] [*URLs*]

The **curl** command hits a URL and downloads the data to a file or standard output. It's great for capturing web pages or downloading files. For example, let's capture the Yahoo home page:

→ **curl** http://www.yahoo.com > mypage.html

which is saved to a file *mypage.html* in the current directory. If you provide multiple URLs, they'll all be appended to *mypage.html*.

Perhaps the most useful feature of **curl** is its ability to download files without needing a web browser:

→ **curl** -O http://www.example.com/files/manual.pdf

You can write shell scripts to download sets of files if you know their names. (See "Programming with Shell Scripts" on page 194

---

for details.) This line downloads files *1.mpeg* through *3.mpeg* from example.com:

```
→ for i in 1 2 3; do \
  curl -o $i.mpeg http://example.com/$i.mpeg; done
```

curl can resume a large download if it gets interrupted in the middle, say, due to a network failure: just run curl -C with the same target URL in the following way:

```
→ curl -o myfile http://example.com/some_big_file
```
Transfer gets interrupted. Now run:
```
→ cat myfile | curl -C - -o myfile \
  http://example.com/some_big_file
```

This sends the partial *myfile* to curl for analysis, then resumes the download. curl has over 100 options, so we'll cover just a few important ones.

Useful options

-o *filename*	Write the retrieved data to the given file. Otherwise it's written to standard output.
-O	Write the retrieved data to a file with the same name as the original.
-K *filename*	Read commands from a configuration file. For example, you can read URLs from the given file and retrieve them in turn, if each line is of the file of the form url="http://...".
-C	Continue mode: if a previous retrieval was interrupted, leaving only a partial file as a result, pick up where curl left off. See the earlier text for a full explanation.
--retry *N*	Try *N* times before giving up.
-s	Silent operation. Do not display anything (including the standard progress meter) while downloading.
-F *name=value*	If the target URL has a form on it, fill in the form values and submit the form, then retrieve the resulting page. For example, if the page has an HTML text input named email, run (say):

```
            curl -F
                              email=smith@example.com
                          .
-m N                   Quit after N seconds of operation.
```

---

wget   stdin   stdout   - file   -- opt   --help   --version

wget [options] URL

The wget command, like curl, hits a URL and downloads the data to a file. Unlike curl, it can also download multiple files and even entire website hierarchies to arbitrary depth.

Getting wget

wget is not supplied with OS X, but it's so powerful and useful that we cover it anyway. If you install the Homebrew package manager, as we explain in "Installing Software with a Package Manager" on page 187, you can obtain wget with a single command:

→ brew install wget

For example, let's capture the Yahoo home page with wget:

```
→ wget http://www.yahoo.com
23:19:51 (220.84 KB/s) - `index.html' saved [31434]
```

which is saved to a file *index.html* in the current directory. wget has the added ability to resume a download if it gets interrupted in the middle, say, due to a network failure: just run wget -c with the same URL and it picks up where it left off. This is simpler than the same feature in curl.

wget can also download files over a network without needing a web browser:

```
→ wget http://www.example.com/files/manual.pdf
```

This is great for large files like videos and disk images. You can also download all pages of a website to a specified depth (say, 2 levels deep), a feat that curl cannot do:

→ `wget -r -l2 http://www.example.com`

wget has over 70 options, so we'll cover just a few important ones.

Useful options

`-i` *filename*	Read URLs from the given file and retrieve them in turn.
`-O` *filename*	Write all the captured HTML to the given file, one page appended after the other.
`-c`	Continue mode: if a previous retrieval was interrupted, leaving only a partial file as a result, pick up where wget left off. That is, if wget had downloaded 100K of a 150K file, the `-c` option says to retrieve only the remaining 50K and append it to the existing file. wget can be fooled, however, if the remote file has changed since the first (partial) download, so use this option only if you know the remote file hasn't changed.
`-t` *N*	Try *N* times before giving up. $N = 0$ means try forever.
`--progress=dot`	Print dots to show the download progress.
`--progress=bar`	Print bars to show the download progress.
`--spider`	Don't download, just check existence of remote pages.
`-nd`	Retrieve all files into the current directory, even if remotely they are in a more complex directory tree. (By default, wget duplicates the remote directory hierarchy.)
`-r`	Retrieve a page hierarchy recursively, including subdirectories.
`-l` *N*	Retrieve files at most *N* levels deep (5 by default).
`-k`	Inside retrieved files, modify URLs so the files can be viewed locally in a web browser.
`-p`	Download all necessary files to make a page display completely, such as stylesheets and images.
`-L`	Follow relative links (within a page) but not absolute links.
`-A` *pattern*	Accept mode: download only files whose names match a given pattern. Patterns may contain the same wildcards as the shell.
`-R` *pattern*	Reject mode: download only files whose names *do not* match a given pattern.

| `-I` *pattern* | Directory inclusion: download files only from directories that match a given pattern. |
| `-X` *pattern* | Directory exclusion: download files only from directories that *do not* match a given pattern. |

Messaging

`talk`	Simple chat program.
`write`	Send messages to a terminal.
`mesg`	Prohibit `talk` and `write`.
`tty`	Print your terminal device name.

Long before instant messaging and texting was invented, users sent messages to each other with older commands that still exist in OS X. These include **talk** and **write**, which work over OS X terminal devices (ttys). This style of communication may seem primitive, but occasionally it can be useful, particularly in pipelines.

---

talk   **stdin**   **stdout**   -file   --opt   --help   --version

```
talk [user[@host]] [tty]
```

The **talk** program predates modern instant messaging by a few decades: it connects two users, logged in on the same or different hosts, for one-to-one communication. (Provided the remote machine accepts talk connections.) It runs in a Terminal window, splitting it horizontally, so you can see your own typing and that of your partner:

→ `talk friend@example.com`

If your partner has multiple login shells running, you can specify one of his ttys for the **talk** connection.

---

write   stdin   **stdout**   - file   -- opt   --help   --version

```
write user [tty]
```

The write program is more primitive than talk: it sends lines of text from one logged-in user to another on the same Mac. It cannot communicate over a network:

```
→ write smith
Hi, how are you?
See you later.
^D
```

^D ends the connection. write is also useful in pipelines for quick one-off messages:

```
→ echo 'Howdy!' | write smith
```

---

mesg   stdin   **stdout**   - file   -- opt   --help   --version

```
mesg [y|n]
```

The mesg program controls whether talk and write connections can reach your terminal. mesg y permits them, mesg n denies them, and mesg prints the current status (y or n). The default is y:

```
→ mesg
is y
→ mesg n            Change the status
→ mesg
is n
```

---

tty   stdin   stdout   - file   -- opt   **--help**   **--version**

```
tty
```

The tty program prints the name of the terminal device associated with the current shell:

```
→ tty
/dev/ttys000
```

Screen Output

echo	Print simple text on standard output.
printf	Print formatted text on standard output.
pbcopy	Copy standard input to the clipboard.
pbpaste	Copy the clipboard to standard output.
yes	Print repeated text on standard output.
clear	Clear the screen or window.

Terminal provides several commands for printing messages on standard output, such as echo:

```
→ echo hello world
hello world
```

Each command has different strengths and intended purposes. These commands are invaluable for learning about the shell, debugging problems, writing shell scripts (see "Programming with Shell Scripts" on page 194), or just talking to yourself.

---

echo   stdin **stdout** -file --opt --help --version

echo [*options*] *strings*

The echo command simply prints its arguments:

```
→ echo We are having fun
We are having fun
```

OS X has several different echo commands with slightly different behavior. There's */bin/echo*, but shells typically override this with a built-in command called echo. To find out which you're using, run the command type echo.

Useful options

-n   Don't print a final newline character.

-e   Recognize and interpret escape characters. (Not supported by */bin/echo*.) For example, try echo 'hello\a' and echo -e 'hello\a'. The first prints literally and the second makes a beep.

-E   Don't interpret escape characters: the opposite of -e. (Not supported by */bin/echo*.)

Available escape characters are:

\a	Alert (play a beep)
\b	Backspace
\c	Don't print the final newline (same effect as -n)
\f	Form feed
\n	Line feed (newline)
\r	Carriage return
\t	Horizontal tab
\v	Vertical tab
\\	A backslash
\'	Single quote
\"	Double quote
\nnn	The character whose ASCII value is *nnn* in octal

---

printf

stdin   **stdout**   - file   **-- opt**   --help   --version

printf *format_string* [*arguments*]

The printf command is an enhanced echo: it prints formatted strings on standard output. It operates much like the C programming language function printf( ), which applies a format string to a sequence of arguments to create some specified output. For example:

```
→ printf "User %s is %d years old.\n" sandy 29
User sandy is 29 years old.
```

The first argument is the format string, which in our example contains two format specifications, %s and %d. The subsequent arguments, sandy and 29, are substituted by printf into the format string and then printed. Format specifications can get fancy with floating-point numbers:

```
→ printf "That\'ll be $%0.2f, sir.\n" 3
That'll be $3.00, sir.
```

It is your responsibility to make sure the number of format specifications (%) equals the number of arguments supplied to `printf` after the format string. If you have too many arguments, the extras are ignored, and if you have too few, `printf` assumes default values (0 for numeric formats, an empty string for string formats). Nevertheless, you should treat such mismatches as errors, even though `printf` is forgiving. If they lurk in your shell scripts, they are bugs waiting to happen.

Format specifications are described in detail on the manpage for the C function `printf` (see `man 3 printf`). Here are some useful ones:

`%d`	Decimal integer
`%ld`	Long decimal integer
`%o`	Octal integer
`%x`	Hexadecimal integer
`%f`	Floating point
`%lf`	Double-precision floating point
`%c`	A single character
`%s`	String
`%q`	String with any shell metacharacters escaped
`%%`	A percent sign by itself

Just after the leading percent sign, you can insert a numeric expression for the minimum width of the output. For example, "%5d" means to print a decimal number in a five-character-wide field, and "%6.2f" means a floating-point number in a six-character-wide field with two digits after the decimal point. Some useful numeric expressions are:

n	Minimum width n.
$0n$	Minimum width n, padded with leading zeroes.
$n.m$	Minimum width n, with m digits after the decimal point.

`printf` also interprets escape characters like "\n" (print a newline character) and "\a" (ring the bell). See the `echo` command for the full list.

---

pbcopy [*options*]

pbcopy copies standard input to the Macintosh clipboard.[20] This is great for copying the output of commands into other programs. For example, to copy the output of who into TextEdit, first send the output to the clipboard:

   → who | pbcopy

Then perform a paste operation in TextEdit. You can also copy the entire contents of a text file to the clipboard with:

   → pbcopy < myfile.txt

Typed without arguments, pbcopy reads from standard input until you type ^D on a line by itself:

```
→ pbcopy
This is the symphony
that Schubert wrote
and never finished.
^D                Ctrl-D to end the input
→
```

Now perform a paste operation in another application, and you'll get the typed text.

pbcopy is most effective when you're using the Mac desktop and Terminal. If you're logged in from a remote system via SSH (as described in "Running a Shell Remotely" on page 183), you won't have the same clipboard as the graphical applications on the desktop, so copying from them won't work.

pbpaste [*options*]

pbpaste is the companion to pbcopy: it copies the contents of the Macintosh clipboard to standard output. For example, to count the number of words in a TextEdit document, copy the document's text to the clipboard and then run:

---

20. Apple uses the term "pasteboard," hence the "pb" in the name.

```
→ pbpaste | wc -w
94821
```

Run without any arguments, pbpaste simply prints the clipboard contents on standard output (onscreen). To copy the contents to a text file, run:

```
→ pbpaste > outfile.txt
```

If you're bored, try this useless pipe command:

```
→ pbpaste | pbcopy
```

which copies the clipboard back into itself. As with pbcopy, to get the most out of pbpaste, you should be using the desktop and Terminal, not logged in from a remote system via SSH.

---

yes

stdin   **stdout**   - file   -- opt   --help   --version

yes [*string*]

The yes command prints the given string (or "y" by default) forever, one string per line:

```
→ yes
y
y
y
...
→ yes again
again
again
again
...
```

Though it might seem useless at first glance, yes can be perfect for turning interactive commands into batch commands. Want to get rid of an annoying "Are you SURE you want to do that" message? Pipe the output of yes into the input of the command to answer all those prompts:

```
→ yes | some interactive command
```

When the interactive command terminates, so will yes. *Be careful* with this technique: you must be certain that every prompt should be answered with the same string.

---

clear

```
clear
```

This command simply clears your shell display.

Math and Calculations

expr	Evaluate simple math on the command line.
dc	Text-based calculator.
seq	Print a sequence of numbers on standard output.

Need a calculator? While the Finder provides a graphical calculator, the Terminal also has some command-line programs to compute mathematical truths for you.

expr

```
expr expression
```

The expr command does simple math (and other expression evaluation) on the command line:

```
→ expr 7 + 3
10
→ expr '(' 7 + 3 ')' '*' 14        We quote special shell characters
140
→ expr length ABCDEFG
7
→ expr 15 '>' 16
0                                  Meaning false
```

Each argument must be separated by whitespace. Notice that we had to quote or escape any characters that have special meaning to the shell. Parentheses (escaped) may be used for grouping. Operators for expr include:

Operator	Numeric operation	String operation
+	Addition	
-	Subtraction	

Operator	Numeric operation	String operation
*	Multiplication	
/	Integer division	
%	Remainder (modulo)	
<	Less than	Earlier in dictionary.
<=	Less than or equal	Earlier in dictionary, or equal.
>	Greater than	Later in dictionary.
>=	Greater than or equal	Later in dictionary, or equal.
=	Equality	Equality.
!=	Inequality	Inequality.
|	Boolean "or"	Boolean "or".
&	Boolean "and"	Boolean "and".
s : regexp		Does the regular expression regexp match string s?

In Boolean expressions, **expr** treats the number 0 and the empty string as false; any other value is true. When returning Boolean results, **expr** returns 0 for false and 1 for true.

expr is not very efficient, but it's highly useful in shell scripts, described in "Programming with Shell Scripts" on page 194. For more complex needs, consider using a language like Perl instead.

---

dc
                        stdin   stdout   - file   -- opt   --help   --version

dc [options] [files]

The **dc** (desk calculator) command is a reverse-polish notation (RPN), stack-based calculator that reads expressions from standard input and writes results to standard output. If you know how to use a Hewlett-Packard RPN calculator, **dc** is pretty easy once you understand its syntax. But if you're used to traditional calculators, **dc** may seem inscrutable. We'll cover only some basic commands.

For stack and calculator operations:

---

q	Quit dc.
f	Print the entire stack.
c	Delete (clear) the entire stack.
p	Print the topmost value on the stack.
P	Pop (remove) the topmost value from the stack.
n k	Set precision of future operations to be *n* decimal places (default is 0: integer operations).

To pop the top two values from the stack, perform a requested operation, and push the result:

+	Addition.
–	Subtraction.
*	Multiplication.
/	Division.
%	Remainder.
^	Exponentiation (second-to-top value is the base, top value is the exponent).

To pop the top value from the stack, perform a requested operation, and push the result:

v	Square root.

Examples:

```
→ dc
4 5 + p          Print the sum of 4 and 5
9
2 3 ^ p          Raise 2 to the 3rd power and print the result
8
10 * p           Multiply the stack top by 10 and print the result
80
f                Print the stack
80
9
+p               Pop the top two stack values and print their sum
89
```

seq

seq [*options*] *specification*

The seq command prints a sequence of integers or real numbers, suitable for piping to other programs. There are three kinds of specification arguments:

A single number: an upper limit
> seq begins at 1 and counts up to the number:
>
> ```
> → seq 3
> 1
> 2
> 3
> ```

Two numbers: lower and upper limit
> seq begins at the first number and counts as far as it can without passing the second number:
>
> ```
> → seq 2 5
> 2
> 3
> 4
> 5
> ```

Three numbers: lower limit, increment, and upper limit
> seq begins at the first number, increments by the second number, and stops at (or before) the third number:
>
> ```
> → seq 1 .3 2
> 1
> 1.3
> 1.6
> 1.9
> ```
>
> You can also go backward with a negative increment:
>
> ```
> → seq 5 -1 2
> 5
> 4
> 3
> 2
> ```

Useful options

-w   Print leading zeroes, as necessary, to give all lines the same width:

```
→ seq -w 8 10
08
09
10
```

-f *format*   Format the output lines with a `printf`-like format string, which must include either %g (the default), %e, or %f:

```
→ seq -f '**%g**' 3
**1**
**2**
**3**
```

-s *string*   Use the given string as a separator between the numbers. By default, a newline is printed (i.e., one number per line):

```
→ seq -s ':' 10
1:2:3:4:5:6:7:8:9:10
```

Dates and Times

cal   Print a calendar.

date   Print or set the date and time.

Need a date? How about a good time? Try these programs to display and set dates and times on your system.

---

cal   stdin   **stdout**   - file   -- opt   --help   --version

cal [*options*] [*month* [*year*]]

The cal command prints a calendar—by default, the current month:

```
→ cal
   December 2011
Su Mo Tu We Th Fr Sa
             1  2  3
 4  5  6  7  8  9 10
11 12 13 14 15 16 17
18 19 20 21 22 23 24
25 26 27 28 29 30 31
```

To print a different calendar, supply a month and four-digit year:

```
→ cal 8 2012
```

If you omit the month (cal 2012), the entire year is printed. You must provide the full year number with four digits: cal 12 will print a calendar for the year 12 A.D.

Useful options

-y   Print the current year's calendar.

-j   Number each day by its position in the year; in our example, September 1 would be displayed as 244, September 2 as 245, and so on.

---

date

date [*options*] [*format*]

The date command prints dates and times. The results will depend on your system's locale settings (for your country and language). In this section we assume an English, US-based locale.

By default, date prints the system date and time in the local time zone:

```
→ date
Wed Mar 14 00:31:53 EDT 2012
```

You can format the output differently by supplying a format string beginning with a plus sign:

```
→ date '+%D'
03/14/12
→ date '+The time is %l:%M %p on a beautiful %A in %B'
The time is 12:31 AM on a beautiful Wednesday in March
```

Here is a sampling of the date command's many formats:

Format	Meaning	Example (US English)
Whole dates and times:		
%c	Full date and time, 12-hour clock	Sun 28 Sep 2003, 09:01:25 PM EDT
%D	Numeric date, 2-digit year	09/28/03
%x	Numeric date, 4-digit year	09/28/2003
%T	Time, 24-hour clock	21:01:25

Format	Meaning	Example (US English)
%X	Time, 12-hour clock	09:01:25 PM
Words:		
%a	Day of week (abbreviated)	Sun
%A	Day of week (complete)	Sunday
%b	Month name (abbreviated)	Sep
%B	Month name (complete)	September
%Z	Time zone	EDT
%p	AM or PM	PM
Numbers:		
%w	Day of week (0–6, 0=Sunday)	0
%u	Day of week (1–7, 1=Monday)	7
%d	Day of month, leading zero	02
%e	Day of month, leading blank	2
%j	Day of year, leading zeroes	005
%m	Month number, leading zero	09
%y	Year, 2 digits	03
%Y	Year, 4 digits	2003
%M	Minute, leading zero	09
%S	Seconds, leading zero	05
%l	Hour, 12-hour clock, leading blank	9
%I	Hour, 12-hour clock, leading zero	09
%k	Hour, 24-hour clock, leading blank	9
%H	Hour, 24-hour clock, leading zero	09
%s	Seconds since the beginning of OS X time: midnight of January 1, 1970	1331699686
Other:		
%n	Newline character	
%t	Tab character	
%%	Percent sign	%

This concludes our documentation of shell commands. Many other commands live in the directories */bin*, */usr/bin*, */sbin*, and */usr/sbin*, so feel free to explore them and learn their features with the man command. Additionally, you can download and install powerful new commands from the Internet, and even create your own by combining other commands. That's what we'll cover next.

CHAPTER 3

Advanced Topics

Our tour of the Macintosh Terminal has shown you a variety of commands, but they are just the tip of the iceberg. In this final part of the book, we'll cover some advanced features to give you even more flexibility and control over your Mac:

Remote logins
> Logging in to your Macintosh from a remote location and running shells without the Terminal.

Package management
> Downloading and installing additional commands from the Internet.

Shell scripts
> Combinations of commands that you can run as a single command.

Running a Shell Remotely

It's possible to log in to a Macintosh over a network—from another Mac, a Windows PC, a Linux box—and run a shell to do work. This is accomplished with software called SSH (Secure Shell) included with OS X. We saw SSH in "Network Connections" on page 157, but only for connecting from your Mac to remote machines. Now we'll see how to log into your Mac from the outside world and run shells. This is a terrific feature if you don't need the Finder or other graphical programs. Multiple users can even log in at the same time from remote locations and run shells simultaneously.

We'll begin by covering the basics of accessing your Macintosh remotely to run shells. Afterward, we'll discuss some roadblocks that can prevent incoming connections from working.

Enabling remote logins

Before connecting to your Macintosh remotely, you need to permit the Mac to receive SSH connections by enabling the Remote Login feature. Be aware that Remote Login and SSH can potentially expose your Macintosh to intruders; however, SSH is considered an industry-standard secure technology by corporations worldwide, so it's a pretty common choice for remote access.[1]

To enable Remote Login on your Mac:

1. Launch the System Preferences application.
2. Click the Sharing icon, and unlock the Sharing Preferences if needed (you'll be prompted for an administrator username and password).
3. Locate the checkbox *Remote Login* and check it. This immediately launches an SSH server in the background.
4. In the *Allow access* section, select either *All users* or *Only these users*, depending on what you want. If the latter, list the users who may access this Mac remotely.
5. Exit the System Preferences application. The SSH server is running and will automatically start up each time you boot your Mac. To disable it, uncheck *Remote Login*.

To test that Remote Login is working, open Terminal and type the following command, which connects from your Mac back to itself using SSH:

---

1. Nevertheless, computer security is a complex topic, so if you have any doubts about permitting SSH access, speak with an expert.

```
→ ssh localhost
```

If you see this scary-looking message, enter "yes":[2]

```
The authenticity of host 'localhost' can't be established.
RSA key fingerprint is 0a:41:c6:ef:66:38:4c:d2:91:e1:…
Are you sure you want to continue connecting (yes/no)? yes
```

This message, which should disappear once you've typed "yes," also means Remote Login is working. Now you should see a password prompt. Type ^C to kill ssh and get your prompt back:

```
Password: ^C
→
```

You are now set up for remote logins. On the other hand, if you see this error message after running ssh:

```
→ ssh localhost
ssh: connect to host localhost port 22: Connection refused
```

then Remote Login isn't running or is misconfigured. Go back and check the earlier setup steps.

Logging in remotely with SSH

Once your Macintosh has Remote Login enabled, try logging into it from another computer. From a Macintosh or a Linux machine, run this command:

```
→ ssh username@hostname
```

where *username* is your username on the destination (your Macintosh), and *hostname* is its hostname or IP address. Enter your password (on the destination Mac) when prompted by SSH, and then you should see a shell prompt.[3]You are remotely

---

2. But only in this special situation, where you are connecting to your own computer (localhost) for the first time! In other situations, this warning can mean a real security problem.

3. You might also see another "RSA key fingerprint" warning, as in "Enabling remote logins" on page 184. If you're positive that you're connecting to your Mac, and not an intruder's machine, you can dismiss this warning as well.

logged in to your Mac! Go ahead and type some commands. When you're finished, type ^D or **exit** to end the shell, logging yourself out and terminating the SSH connection. We discuss the **ssh** command in more detail in "Network Connections" on page 157.

To connect from a Windows PC to your Macintosh via SSH, you'll need an SSH client program for Windows. A simple, free program is PuTTY, which you can download from *http://www .chiark.greenend.org.uk/~sgtatham/putty/*. Provide the hostname of your Macintosh to PuTTY, you'll be prompted for your Mac username and password, and then a shell will run.

SSH roadblocks

When connecting to a Macintosh remotely via SSH, you can run into difficulty and connections may fail. Here are some common reasons:

Remote Login via SSH not enabled
> The Macintosh must be configured to enable Remote Login via SSH, as described in "Enabling remote logins" on page 184.

SSH configuration issues
> SSH servers are highly configurable via the file */etc/ sshd_config*. Some configurations can deny remote connections in certain situations. See **man sshd_config** to learn more.

Firewalls
> If your Macintosh is behind a firewall, say, inside a company's private network, you might not be able to connect to it. (The Mac's own Firewall application will not interfere with Remote Login.)

Dynamic IP addresses
> Your Macintosh's internet service provider might change the Mac's IP address on a regular basis. (In technical terms, your Mac is using DHCP to obtain its IP address.) If so, and you don't know the current IP address, you

won't be able to connect to your Mac from the outside. This is common for home computer setups. You can get around this issue by signing up for a dynamic DNS service, such as Dyn (*http://www.dyn.com*), that assigns a consistent hostname to your Mac that you can use externally.

Installing Software with a Package Manager

You can install thousands of new commands for use within the Terminal. The method of installation is different from what you've seen in the point-and-click world, where you run a graphical installer or drag icons into your *Applications* folder. Instead, you use a program called a *package manager*, which itself runs on the command line. Setting up a package manager is a multi-step process, but when it's complete, you'll be able to install new commands extremely easily.[4] We will lead you through the basic steps:

1. Obtain a free Apple Developer ID at *http://developer.apple .com*. (You don't have to be a software developer to get an ID.)

2. Download and install Xcode, Apple's software development application.

3. Download and install the Command Line Tools for Xcode.

4. Download and install Homebrew, a convenient, free package manager.

Once these steps are complete, you can install new command-line programs easily with Homebrew, by typing the command `brew install`.

---

4. Frankly, setting up a package manager on the Mac is tedious, inconvenient, error-prone, and overall a pain in the neck. (Much more difficult than similar setups in the Windows and Linux world.) But the end result is definitely worthwhile and we recommend it.

Obtaining an Apple Developer ID

An Apple Developer ID is a free login account on the website *developer.apple.com*. You'll need this account to download necessary software for installing new command-line tools. Simply visit *developer.apple.com* and sign up.

Installing Xcode

Xcode is a package for developing software for Apple products, including the Macintosh, iPhone, iPad, and more. Even if you're not a software developer, you need Xcode as a prerequisite for the package manager.

As of OS X Lion, Xcode is a free download from the App Store.[5] Simply search for "Xcode" and download the application. When the Xcode icon appears on your desktop, launch it and follow the installation prompts. When the installation is complete, Xcode is now located in your *Applications* folder.

Installing Command Line Tools for Xcode

Next, install the command line tools for Xcode. In modern versions of Xcode, the installation is done within Xcode. For example, in OS X Lion, launch Xcode, visit its Xcode menu, and choose Preferences. When the Preferences window opens, click the Downloads pane, locate Command Line Tools, and click Install. [6] When installation is finished, you're ready to install Homebrew and make package management simple.

As an aside, if you're a software developer, you'll be delighted that the Command Line Tools for Xcode include compilers and

---

5. For older versions of OS X, download and install Xcode from *developer.apple.com*. Get Xcode version 3.2.6 for Snow Leopard, 3.1.4 for Leopard, 2.5 for Tiger, or 1.5 for Panther. Some versions of OS X might also include Xcode on their installation DVDs.

6. For older versions of Xcode, or if you encounter errors during this installation (as this author did), download the Command Line Tools for Xcode directly from *developer.apple.com*.

debuggers (the GNU C Compiler and GNU Debugger, Make, Flex, Bison, etc.), revision control systems (Subversion, Git, CVS, RCS), and more. Most of them get installed in */usr/bin*.

Installing the Homebrew Package Manager

Homebrew is a free application that simplifies the process of installing command-line tools. With a single command, you can search for, install, uninstall, or update any of thousands of free tools. To install Homebrew:

1. Visit *http://mxcl.github.com/homebrew/* and follow links to the installation instructions.

2. Open a Terminal window on your Mac.

3. The Homebrew installation instructions will provide you with a long, cryptic command (beginning with **/usr/bin/ ruby...**). Copy and paste this command into the shell in your Terminal window, and press Enter.

4. As the installation command runs in the shell, it will prompt you with questions. Respond to them in the shell. When the installation completes, you'll have a new command available in the shell, **brew**, for installing and managing software packages.

5. Run the **brew doctor** command, which validates that Homebrew is properly installed:

   → **brew doctor**

   If you see any error messages, read them carefully and correct whatever problems are reported. For example, this message:

   `Error: no such file or directory - /usr/local/Cellar`

   indicates a directory is missing, so you'd run **mkdir /usr/ local/Cellar** to create it. Keep rerunning **brew doctor** until there are no errors and you see this message:

   → **brew doctor**
   `Your system is raring to brew.`

indicating that the installation is correct and complete.

Guess what? You are finally done! After all that work installing Xcode, the Command Line Tools, and Homebrew, you now have a simple package manager for downloading and installing new commands. Hooray!

Using Homebrew

The `brew` command performs all Homebrew operations: searching for software, installing it, updating it, uninstalling it, and more. Let's demonstrate its use by installing a package.[7] Suppose you want a command to work with MP3 files, displaying and modifying the artist and title information inside them, known as *ID3 tags*. We use Homebrew to search for any packages with "id3" in their names:

```
→ brew search id3
id3lib      id3tool     id3v2      libid3tag
```

After some web research, you determine that `id3tool` is the program you want. To install it, run the `brew install` command:

```
→ brew install id3tool
==> Downloading http://nekohako.xware.cx/id3tool/...
############################################################
==> ./configure --disable-debug --prefix=/usr/local/...
==> make install
/usr/local/Cellar/id3tool/1.2a: 6 files, 40K,
built in 2 seconds
```

That's it! The `id3tool` command is now installed, which you can confirm with the `brew list` command:

```
→ brew list | grep id3tool
id3tool
```

and you can see the location where it got installed, using the shell's `type` command:

---

7. Homebrew uses the term *formula* instead of "package."

```
→ type id3tool
/usr/local/bin/id3tool
```

You can now run **id3tool** to examine your MP3 files:

```
→ id3tool song.mp3
Filename: song.mp3
Song Title:    Playing The Game
Artist:        Gentle Giant
Album:         The Power And The Glory
Track:         4
Year:          1974
Genre:         Progressive Rock (0x5C)
```

Here is a list of common **brew** commands for managing software packages:

Action	Homebrew command
Search for a package that meets your needs.	brew search *part_of_package_name* brew search */regular_expression/*
List all packages that Homebrew can install.	brew search
Check if a package is installed.	brew list | grep *package_name*
Download and install a package.	brew install *package_name*
Download a package without installing it.	brew fetch *package_name*
Learn about a package, whether installed or not.	brew info *package_name*
Visit the home page for a particular package to learn more about it.	brew home *package_name*
List the contents of an installed package.	brew list *package_name*
Update an installed package.	brew upgrade *package_name*
Remove an installed package.	brew uninstall *package_name*
List all packages installed on the system.	brew list
Update all installed packages to their latest version. (Also updates Homebrew itself.)	brew update

Action	Homebrew command
List common brew commands.	`brew help`
Visit the Homebrew home page (opens a browser window).	`brew home`
Validate that Homebrew is installed correctly.	`brew doctor`

Homebrew has many other features, including the ability to create packages of your own. See the manpage for details. In addition, Homebrew is not the only package manager available for OS X. If you'd like to explore others, try Fink (*http://www.finkproject.org/*) or MacPorts (*http://www.macports.org/*).

Installing from TAR Files

Package managers like Homebrew are not the only means for installing software on the command line. Much free software is distributed in compressed TAR files, which we first encountered in "File Compression and Packaging" on page 102. You can work with these files manually to unpack, build, and install programs without a package manager. However, you'll need to deal yourself with dependencies between programs, difficult uninstalls, and a host of other issues that package managers handle automatically. (In fact, Homebrew uses compressed TAR files behind the scenes.) Let's examine how to work with these files.

Packaged software files with names ending in *.tar.gz* and *.tar.bz2* typically contain source code written in a programming language.[8] Before installing the software, you'll need to compile (build) it. Typical build instructions are:

1. List the package contents, one file per line. Assure yourself that each file, when extracted, won't overwrite something precious on your system, either accidentally or maliciously:[9]

---

8. The extension *.tar.gz* is sometimes shortened to *.tgz*.

```
→ tar tvzf package.tar.gz | less        For gzip files
→ tar tvjf package.tar.bz2 | less       For bzip2 files
```

2. If satisfied, extract the files into a new directory. Run these commands as yourself, not as root, for safety reasons:

```
→ mkdir newdir
→ cd newdir
→ tar xvzf <path>/package.tar.gz         For gzip files
→ tar xvjf <path>/package.tar.bz2        For bzip2 files
```

3. Look for an extracted file named *INSTALL* or *README*. Read it to learn how to build the software, for example:

```
→ cd newdir
→ less INSTALL
```

4. Usually the *INSTALL* or *README* file will tell you to run a script called **configure** in the current directory, then run make, then run make install. Examine the options you may pass to the **configure** script:

```
→ ./configure --help
```

Run **configure** with appropriate options:

```
→ ./configure options...
```

then run make to build the binary program from the source files:

```
→ make
```

and finally, run make install as an administrator to install the software into system folders:

```
→ sudo make install
Password: *******
```

Now your new software is ready for use.

---

9. A maliciously designed TAR file could include an absolute file path like */etc/passwd* designed to overwrite your system password file.

Programming with Shell Scripts

For our final topic in this book, we'll show you how to combine multiple commands to perform more complex operations. Earlier when we covered the shell (bash), we said it had a programming language built in. In fact, you can write programs, or *shell scripts*, to accomplish tasks that a single command cannot. Like any good programming language, the shell has variables, conditionals (if-then-else), loops, input and output, and more. Entire books have been written on shell scripting, so we'll be covering the bare minimum to get you started. For full documentation, run `info bash`, search the Web, or pick up a more in-depth O'Reilly book.

Creating and Running Shell Scripts

To create a shell script, simply put bash commands into a file as you would type them. For example, you could put these lines into a file called *myscript*:

```
echo "Here are your files:"
ls
```

When you run the script, its commands will run in order:

```
Here are your files:
file1.txt    file2.pdf
```

There are several ways to run a shell script:

Prepend `#!/bin/bash` *and make the file executable*
> This is the most common way to run scripts. Add the following line to the top of the script file:
>
> ```
> #!/bin/bash
> ```
>
> It must be the first line of the file, left-justified. The result in our example looks like this:
>
> ```
> #!/bin/bash
> echo "Here are your files:"
> ls
> ```
>
> Then make the file executable:

> → `chmod +x myscript`

Move it into a directory in your search path. Then run it like any other command:

> → `myscript`

Alternatively, run the script from your current directory by prepending "./" (indicating the current directory) so the shell finds the script:

> → `./myscript`

The current directory is generally not in your search path for security reasons. You wouldn't want a local script named, say, "ls" to override the real `ls` command unexpectedly.

Pass to bash

You can run bash directly as a command. It will interpret its argument as the name of a script and run it:

> → `bash myscript`

Run in current shell with "." or `source`

The preceding methods run your script as an independent entity that has no effect on your current shell.[10] If you want your script to make changes to your current shell (setting variables, changing directory, and so on), it can be run in the current shell with the `source` or "." command, since the two are equivalent:

> → `. myscript`
> → `source myscript`

Launch from the Finder

If you make a script executable with `chmod`, it can be run from the Finder by double-clicking on its icon:[11]

---

10. That's because the script runs in a separate shell (a *subshell* or *child shell*) that cannot alter the original shell.

11. In OS X versions prior to 10.5, scripts need an additional step to be launchable from the Finder. Either rename the script to have the extension *.command* (e.g., *myscript.command*), or open the script's Info dialog (⌘I) and set it to open with Terminal.

```
→ chmod +x myscript
```

After the script runs, a Terminal window might be left around that you have to close by hand. You can change this behavior so the window closes when the shell exits:

1. In the Terminal menu, choose *Preferences...* to make the Preferences dialog appear.

2. Click the *Settings* icon.

3. Click the *Shell* tab.

4. Locate the settings *When the shell exits*, and select the value *Close the window*.

5. Exit the Preferences dialog. When you launch scripts from the Finder, the associated Terminal window will now close automatically.

Now that you know how to run shell scripts, let's discuss the various constructs you can put into these scripts.

Whitespace and Linebreaks

bash shell scripts are sensitive to whitespace and linebreaks. Because the "keywords" of this programming language are actually commands evaluated by the shell, you need to separate arguments with whitespace. Likewise, a linebreak in the middle of a command will mislead the shell into thinking the command is incomplete. Follow the conventions we present here and you should be fine.

If you must break a long command into multiple lines, end each line (except the last) with a single \ character, which means "continued on next line":

```
→ grep abcdefghijklmnopqrstuvwxyz file1 file2 \
  file3 file4
```

The slash must be the final character on its line: that is, you must press Enter immediately after it. Finally, any text following a hash mark (#) on a line is a comment.

Variables

We described shell variables in "Shell variables" on page 29:

```
→ MYVAR=6
→ echo $MYVAR
6
```

All values held in variables are strings, but if they are numeric, the shell will treat them as numbers when appropriate:

```
→ NUMBER="10"
→ expr $NUMBER + 5
15
```

When you refer to a variable's value in a shell script, it's a good idea to surround it with double quotes to prevent certain runtime errors. An undefined variable, or a variable with spaces in its value, will evaluate to something unexpected if not surrounded by quotes, causing your script to malfunction:

```
→ FILENAME="My Document"          Space in the name
→ ls $FILENAME                    Try to list it
ls: My: No such file or directory Oops! ls saw 2 arguments
ls: Document: No such file or directory
→ ls -l "$FILENAME"               List it properly
My Document                       ls saw only 1 argument
```

If a variable name is evaluated adjacent to another string, surround it with curly braces to prevent unexpected behavior:

```
→ NAME="apple"
→ echo "The plural of $NAME is $NAMEs"
The plural of apple is            Oops! No variable "NAMEs"
→ echo  "The plural of $NAME is ${NAME}s"
The plural of apple is apples     What we wanted
```

Input and Output

Script output is provided by the echo and printf commands, which we described in "Screen Output" on page 170:

```
→ echo "Hello world"
Hello world
→ printf "I am %d years old\n" `expr 20 + 20`
I am 40 years old
```

Input is provided by the **read** command, which reads one line from standard input and stores it in a variable:

```
→ read name
Sandy Smith <ENTER>
→ echo "I read the name $name"
I read the name Sandy Smith
```

Booleans and Return Codes

Before we can describe conditionals and loops, we need to explain the concept of a Boolean (true/false) test. A Boolean is an entity that can have the value true or false. A Boolean test simply checks a value to see if it's true or false. To the shell, the value 0 means true or success, and anything else means false or failure. (Think of zero as "no error" and other values as error codes.)[12]

Every command returns an integer value, called a *return code* or *exit status*, to the shell when the command exits. You can see this value in the special variable $?:

```
→ cat myfile
My name is Sandy Smith and
I really like OS X Lion
→ grep Smith myfile                    A match was found...
My name is Sandy Smith and
→ echo $?
0                                      ...so return code is "success"
→ grep aardvark myfile
→ echo $?                              No match was found...
1                                      ...so return code is "failure"
```

The return codes of a command are usually documented on its manpage.

test and "["

The shell's **test** command evaluates simple Boolean expressions involving numbers and strings, setting its exit status to 0 (true) or 1 (false):

---

12. This is the opposite of how the **expr** command treats Booleans.

```
→ test 10 -lt 5          Is 10 less than 5?
→ echo $?
1                        No, it isn't
→ test -n "hello"        Does the string "hello" have nonzero length?
→ echo $?
0                        Yes, it does
```

Here are common **test** arguments for checking properties of integers, strings, and files:

File tests

-d *name*	File *name* is a directory
-f *name*	File *name* is a regular file
-L *name*	File *name* is a symbolic link
-r *name*	File *name* exists and is readable
-w *name*	File *name* exists and is writable
-x *name*	File *name* exists and is executable
-s *name*	File *name* exists and its size is nonzero
f1 -nt *f2*	File *f1* is newer than file *f2*
f1 -ot *f2*	File *f1* is older than file *f2*

String tests

s1 = *s2*	String *s1* equals string *s2*
s1 != *s2*	String *s1* does not equal string *s2*
-z *s1*	String *s1* has zero length
-n *s1*	String *s1* has nonzero length

Numeric tests

a -eq *b*	Integers *a* and *b* are equal
a -ne *b*	Integers *a* and *b* are not equal
a -gt *b*	Integer *a* is greater than integer *b*
a -ge *b*	Integer *a* is greater than or equal to integer *b*
a -lt *b*	Integer *a* is less than integer *b*
a -le *b*	Integer *a* is less than or equal to integer *b*

Combining and negating tests

t1 -a t2	And: both tests t1 and t2 are true
t1 -o t2	Or: either test t1 or t2 is true
! *your_test*	Negate the test, i.e., your_test is false
\(*your_test* \)	Parentheses are used for grouping, as in algebra

test has an unusual alias, "[" (left square bracket), as a short-hand for use with conditionals and loops. If you use this short-hand, you must supply a final argument of "]" (right square bracket) to signify the end of the test. The following tests are identical to the previous two:

```
→ [ 10 -lt 5 ]
→ echo $?
1
→ [ -n "hello" ]
→ echo $?
0
```

Remember that "[" is a command like any other, so it is followed by *individual arguments separated by whitespace*. So if you mistakenly forget some whitespace:

```
→ [ 5 -lt 4]          No space between 4 and ]
bash: [: missing ']'
```

then **test** thinks the final argument is the string "4]" and complains that the final bracket is missing.

true and false

bash has built-in commands **true** and **false**, which simply set their exit status to 0 and 1, respectively:

```
→ true
→ echo $?
0
→ false
→ echo $?
1
```

These will be useful when we discuss conditionals and loops.

Conditionals

A conditional statement provides a way to execute one set of commands or another, based on Boolean tests (or *conditions*). One example is the **if** statement, which chooses between alternatives. The simplest form is the **if-then** statement:

```
if command          If exit status of command is 0
then
  body
fi
```

For example, if you write a script that must be run with **sudo**, you can check for administrator privileges like this:

```
if [ `whoami` = "root" ]
then
  echo "You are the superuser"
fi
```

Here's a practical example for your ~/.bash_profile file (see "Tailoring Shell Behavior" on page 43). Some users like to place some of their shell configuration commands (such as aliases) into a separate file, ~/.bashrc. We can tell ~/.bash_profile to load and run these commands if the file exists:

```
# Inside ~/.bash_profile:
if [ -f $HOME/.bashrc ]
then
  . $HOME/.bashrc
fi
```

Next is the **if-then-else** statement:

```
if command
then
  body1
else
  body2
fi
```

For example:

```
if [ `whoami` = "root" ]
then
  echo "You are the superuser"
else
```

```
  echo "You are an ordinary dude"
fi
```

Finally, we have the form **if-then-elif-else**, which may have as many tests as you like:

```
if command1
then
  body1
elif command2
then
  body2
elif ...
  ...
else
  bodyN
fi
```

For example:

```
if [ `whoami` = "root" ]
then
  echo "You are the superuser"
elif [ "$USER" = "root" ]
then
  echo "You might be the superuser"
elif [ "$bribe" -gt 10000 ]
then
  echo "You can pay to be the superuser"
else
  echo "You are still an ordinary dude"
fi
```

The **case** statement is a simplified alternative to long chains of **if-then-else** if all the Boolean tests use the same value or expression. In this example, the variable value $answer is used by all the choices, so **case** is an appropriate statement:

```
echo "What would you like to do?"
read answer
case "$answer" in
  eat)
    echo "OK, have a hamburger"
    ;;
  sleep)
    echo "Good night then"
    ;;
  *)
```

```
      echo "I'm not sure what you want to do"
      echo "I guess I'll see you tomorrow"
      ;;
  esac
```

The general form is:

```
  case string in
    expr1)
      body1
      ;;
    expr2)
      body2
      ;;
    ...
    exprN)
      bodyN
      ;;
    *)
      bodyelse
      ;;
  esac
```

where *string* is any value, usually a variable value like $answer, and *expr1* through *exprN* are patterns (run the command **info bash reserved case** for details), with the final * like a final "else." Each set of commands must be terminated by ;; (as shown):

```
  case $letter in
    X)
      echo "$letter is an X"
      ;;
    [aeiou])
      echo "$letter is a vowel"
      ;;
    [0-9])
      echo "$letter is a digit, silly"
      ;;
    *)
      echo "The letter '$letter' is not supported"
      ;;
  esac
```

Loops

The **while** loop repeats a set of commands as long as a condition is true:

```
while command                While the exit status of command is 0
do
  body
done
```

For example, if this is the script **myscript**:

```
i=0
while [ $i -lt 3 ]
do
  echo "$i"
  i=`expr $i + 1`
done

→ ./myscript
0
1
2
```

The **until** loop repeats until a condition becomes true:

```
until command                While the exit status of command is nonzero
do
  body
done
```

For example:

```
i=0
until [ $i -ge 3 ]
do
  echo "$i"
  i=`expr $i + 1`
done

→ ./myscript
0
1
2
```

The **for** loop iterates over values from a list:

```
for variable in list
do
```

```
  body
done
```

For example:

```
for name in Tom Jack Harry
do
  echo "$name is my friend"
done
```

```
→ ./myscript
Tom is my friend
Jack is my friend
Harry is my friend
```

The **for** loop is particularly handy for processing lists of files;
for example, all files of a certain type in the current directory:

```
for file in *.doc *.docx
do
  echo "$file is a Microsoft Word file"
done
```

Be careful to avoid infinite loops, using **while** with the condition **true**, or **until** with the condition **false**:

```
while true              Beware: infinite loop!
do
  echo "forever"
done
```

```
until false             Beware: infinite loop!
do
  echo "forever again"
done
```

Use **break** or **exit** to terminate these loops based on some condition inside their bodies.

Break and Continue

The **break** command jumps out of the nearest enclosing loop.
Consider this simple script called **myscript**:

```
for name in Tom Jack Harry
do
  echo $name
  echo "again"
```

```
done
echo "all done"
```

```
→ ./myscript
Tom
again
Jack
again
Harry
again
all done
```

Now with a break:

```
for name in Tom Jack Harry
do
  echo $name
  if [ "$name" = "Jack" ]
  then
    break
  fi
  echo "again"
done
echo "all done"
```

```
→ ./myscript
Tom
again
Jack                 The break occurs after this line
all done
```

The continue command forces a loop to jump to its next
iteration:

```
for name in Tom Jack Harry
do
  echo $name
  if [ "$name" = "Jack" ]
  then
    continue
  fi
  echo "again"
done
echo "all done"
```

```
→ ./myscript
Tom
again
```

```
Jack            The continue occurs after this line
Harry
again
all done
```

break and continue also accept a numeric argument (break *N*, continue *N*) to control multiple layers of loops (e.g., jump out of *N* layers of loops), but this kind of scripting leads to confusing code and we don't recommend it.

Command-Line Arguments

Shell scripts can accept command-line arguments just like other commands.[13] Within a shell script, you can refer to these arguments as $1, $2, $3, and so on:

```
→ cat myscript
#!/bin/bash
echo "My name is $1 and I come from $2"

→ ./myscript Johnson Wisconsin
My name is Johnson and I come from Wisconsin
→ ./myscript Bob
My name is Bob and I come from
```

Your script can test the number of arguments it received with $#:

```
if [ $# -lt 2 ]
then
  echo "$0 error: you must supply two arguments"
else
  echo "My name is $1 and I come from $2"
fi
```

The special value $0 contains the name of the script, and is handy for usage and error messages:

```
→ ./myscript Bob
./myscript error: you must supply two arguments
```

13. To a shell script, there is no difference between an option and an argument. They are all considered arguments.

To iterate over all command-line arguments, use a **for** loop with the special variable $@, which holds all arguments:

```
for arg in $@
do
  echo "I found the argument $arg"
done
```

Exiting with a Return Code

The **exit** command terminates your script and passes a given return code to the shell. Return codes are the reason that commands could be run in sequence in "Combining commands" on page 34: the shell checks the return code of the preceding command before running the next. Also, a shell script that calls another script can check its exit code in conditional statements to determine what to do next.

By tradition, scripts should return 0 for success and 1 (or other nonzero value) on failure. If your script doesn't call **exit**, the return code is automatically 0:

```
if [ $# -lt 2 ]
then
  echo "$0 error: you must supply two arguments"
  exit 1
else
  echo "My name is $1 and I come from $2"
fi
exit 0

→ ./myscript Bob
./myscript error: you must supply two arguments
→ echo $?
1
```

Beyond Shell Scripting

Shell scripts are fine for many purposes, but OS X comes with much more powerful scripting languages, as well as compiled programming languages. Here are a few.

Language	Command	To get started...
C, C++	gcc, g++[a]	man gcc
		http://www.gnu.org/software/gcc/
Perl	perl	man perl
		http://www.perl.com/
PHP	php	man php
		http://www.php.net/
Python	python	man python
		http://www.python.org/
Ruby	ruby	man ruby
		http://ruby-lang.org/
.NET	mono	man mono
		http://www.mono-project.com/Mono:OSX
Java	javac	man javac
		http://java.sun.com/

a. These are not supplied with OS X, but are installed with Xcode.

Getting Help

If you need more information than this book provides, there are several things you can do.

Run the man *command*

The man command displays an online manual page, or *manpage*, for a given program. For example, to learn about listing files with ls, run:

→ man ls

To search for manpages by keyword for a particular topic, use the -k option followed by the keyword:

→ man -k database

Run the `info` *command*

The `info` command is a text-based, menu-driven help system covering some important Terminal commands and applications:

→ `info ls`

While `info` is running, some useful keystrokes are:

- To get help, type h
- To quit, type q
- To page forward and backward, use the space bar and Backspace keys
- To jump between hyperlinks, press Tab
- To follow a hyperlink, press Enter

If `info` has no documentation on a given program, it displays the program's manpage. For a listing of available documentation, type `info` by itself. To learn how to navigate the info system, type `info info`.

Use the `--help` *option (if any)*

Some commands respond to the option `--help` by printing a short help message. Try:

→ `diff --help`

If the output is longer than the screen, pipe it into the `less` program to display it in pages (press q to quit):

→ `diff --help | less`

Examine the directory /usr/share/doc

This directory contains supporting documents for several programs. For example, files for the bash shell are found in */usr/share/doc/bash*.

Mac-specific websites

Some great sites for asking OS X questions are Mac OS X Hints (*http://hintsforums.macworld.com/*) and AskDifferent (*http://apple.stackexchange.com/*). You can also visit the website for this book: *http://shop.oreilly.com/product/0636920025382.do*.

Linux help sites
> Many shell commands are found in Linux as well, so check Linux-related sites, including *http://www.linuxquestions .org*, *http://unix.stackexchange.com*, *http://www.linuxhelp .net*, and *http://www.linuxforums.org*.

Web search
> To decipher an error message from a command, enter the message into a web search engine, word for word, and you will likely find helpful results.

Final Words

We've covered many commands and capabilities of the Terminal and the shell. Nevertheless, we've just scratched the surface. OS X includes over 1,000 commands that can be run in the Terminal, and thousands more can be downloaded and installed. We encourage you to continue reading, exploring, and learning the capabilities of the Macintosh Terminal. Good luck!

Acknowledgments

This book is dedicated with love to my parents who are both Mac fans. My father, Stephen Barrett, is a prolific writer who inspired me to be an author. My mother, Judith Barrett, taught me the value of working hard. Thanks, Mom and Dad: I hope you'll both learn interesting things from this book.

I also thank my editor Andy Oram and long-time collaborator Mike Loukides, and the O'Reilly production staff. The technical review team (Stephen Barrett, Vandad Nahavandipoor, Rich Rosen, Ernie Rothman, and Matthew Stevenson) did an outstanding job and definitely improved the manuscript. Thanks also go to Chris Connors at Vistaprint, and as always, to my amazing and patient family, Lisa and Sophia.

Index

Symbols

We'd like to hear your suggestions for improving our indexes. Send email to *index@oreilly.com*.

Y

yes command, 174

Z

zcat command, 102, 103, 104
zip command, 104

The information you need, when and where you need it.

With Safari Books Online, you can:

Access the contents of thousands of technology and business books

- Quickly search over 7000 books and certification guides
- Download whole books or chapters in PDF format, at no extra cost, to print or read on the go
- Copy and paste code
- Save up to 35% on O'Reilly print books
- **New!** Access mobile-friendly books directly from cell phones and mobile devices

Stay up-to-date on emerging topics before the books are published

- Get on-demand access to evolving manuscripts.
- Interact directly with authors of upcoming books

Explore thousands of hours of video on technology and design topics

- Learn from expert video tutorials
- Watch and replay recorded conference sessions

O'REILLY®

Spreading the knowledge of innovators   oreilly.com

Get even more for your money.

Join the O'Reilly Community, and register the O'Reilly books you own. It's free, and you'll get:

- $4.99 ebook upgrade offer
- 40% upgrade offer on O'Reilly print books
- Membership discounts on books and events
- Free lifetime updates to ebooks and videos
- Multiple ebook formats, DRM FREE
- Participation in the O'Reilly community
- Newsletters
- Account management
- 100% Satisfaction Guarantee

Registering your books is easy:
1. Go to: oreilly.com/go/register
2. Create an O'Reilly login.
3. Provide your address.
4. Register your books.

Note: English-language books only

To order books online:
oreilly.com/store

For questions about products or an order:
orders@oreilly.com

To sign up to get topic-specific email announcements and/or news about upcoming books, conferences, special offers, and new technologies:
elists@oreilly.com

For technical questions about book content:
booktech@oreilly.com

To submit new book proposals to our editors:
proposals@oreilly.com

O'Reilly books are available in multiple DRM-free ebook formats. For more information:
oreilly.com/ebooks

O'REILLY®

Spreading the knowledge of innovators   oreilly.com

Milton Keynes UK
Ingram Content Group UK Ltd.
UKHW032257191024
449882UK00009B/148